Patchwork Table Runners™

Edited by Jeanne Stauffer & Sandra L. Hatch

HOUSE of
WHITE
BIRCHES
PUBLISHERS
SINCE 1947

Patchwork
Table Runners™

Copyright © 2009

DRG
306 East Parr Road
Berne, IN 46711

Editors **Jeanne Stauffer & Sandra L. Hatch**
Art Director **Brad Snow**
Publishing Services Director **Brenda Gallmeyer**

Managing Editor **Dianne Schmidt**
Assistant Art Director **Nick Pierce**
Copy Supervisor **Michelle Beck**
Copy Editors **Angie Buckles, Amanda Ladig,
  Mary O'Donnell**
Technical Artist **Connie Rand**

Graphic Arts Supervisor **Ronda Bechinski**
Book Design **Nick Pierce**
Graphic Artists **Erin Augsburger, Joanne Gonzalez**
Production Assistants **Marj Morgan,
  Judy Neuenschwander**

Photography Supervisor **Tammy Christian**
Photography **Matthew Owen**
Photo Stylist **Tammy Steiner**

Printed in United States of America
First Printing: China 2009
Library of Congress Number: 2008936678
Hardcover ISBN: 978-1-59217-244-3
Softcover ISBN: 978-1-59217-245-0

DRGbooks.com

3456789

Welcome

Table runners are such fun quilting projects to make. They are so small that many times you can make a runner in an evening without making a trip to a quilt shop to buy more fabric.

They are great gifts for almost any occasion. They add zip and color to any room and almost any flat surface. Use them on a coffee table or end table. Place them on a dresser or trunk. If you need an unusual size, we've included a special section on how to change the size of the table runners featured in this book.

If your favorite technique is piecing, you'll find many pleasing patchwork runners in this book. If you love to appliqué, you will love the runners that add a touch of appliqué to the patchwork.

If you are ready to learn something new about quilting, the patterns in the Try a New Technique section are ready and waiting. Learn to create a vintage look, make a reversible runner, use wool, try sashiko stitching, work with fabric strips and more.

Whether you are drawn to runners that have a contemporary look or a vintage look, you'll find the style you like best here. There are quick and easy runners, and runners that show off your skills as an accomplished quilter. You can make runners for everyday use and for special occasions. You'll find it all in these pages!

Enjoy every stitch you make!

Jeanne Stauffer   Janera A Hatch

Contents

Changing the Size of a Table Runner

If the runner you want to make is not the right size to fit your table, don't let that stop you. Read this chapter on easy ways to change the size of a runner, and you will soon be making all your runners fit perfectly.

Changing the Size of a Table Runner

By Jodi Warner

There are many possible reasons why you might want to change the size of a table-runner pattern. The following tips will help you redesign any pattern.

What if a great runner project that has captured your fancy is not sized for your particular table? Or perhaps you plan to use it atop a chest or sideboard, across a piano or as a shelf backdrop and it is too wide, or not wide enough.

Your redesign situation and the final solution you choose may be unique. Here are some practical strategies to show you how.

Tools for Redesigning

Common office supplies and equipment will be very helpful as you customize your table-runner design. Gather these as you begin the process.

- Tracing paper
- Tape measure or yardstick
- Calculator
- Repositionable tape
- Glue stick
- ¼"-gridded graph paper in letter or legal-size sheets
- Fine-lead mechanical pencil (.5mm recommended) and good eraser
- See-through straightedge gridded ruler
- Photocopier with enlargement/ reduction capabilities
- Computer quilt-design program
- Red felt-tip or pencil for final size notations

Determining Runner Target Size

Use a tape measure to find the width and length you want your project to be. How much furniture margin do you wish to leave exposed? As you decide on size, remember to allow for some shrinkage in size due to quilting, as well as for the fractional amounts that the binding edge may add on.

You may wish to consider some common sizes of furniture where runners are typically used.

Dining tables:
4 person 40"–45" square
6 person 44"–48" x 72"–74"
8 person 44"–48" x 92"–94"
Accent table, lowboy, buffet sideboard:
18"–20" deep x 46"–60" long
Square accent table:
58"–60" square
Low bookcase:
12" deep x 30"–56" long
TV stand:
20" deep x 53"–54" long
Piano, spinet or console styles:
11" deep x 54" long

Keep function in mind. If you wish to keep a runner centered on the table during meal service, will there be enough space left on the table for regular set-up of china, crystal and silver? Consider whether a narrower or a wider solution is better. Of course, when a runner is for decorative use only and removed prior to regular table use, this consideration isn't necessary.

If you want a runner to reach the full length of your table, choose whether it will leave a margin of exposed table top, reach to the edge or be several inches longer to hang gracefully over the edge. For this last style, over-hang should be substantial enough to make the downward drop without interfering with dining. Shaping the ends as points with hidden, sewn-in drapery weights or decorative tassels may provide just the right assist.

Changing Length

Consider a strategy: Once you have determined your target length, analyze how the pattern may offer solutions for size change. Following are some simple questions to get the process started, along with a few examples from the projects in this book.

• Will the addition of borders from matching or accent fabrics achieve the desired width or length? Fussy-Cut Floral Stars and Stepping Stones runners are examples where this simple solution would add width and length to the project.

Stepping Stones, page 15

• Are there separate blocks or border elements that can be removed or repeated? For example, eliminate or add a center block to Autumn Leaves & Pumpkins; increase or decrease the number of hourglass units in the center of Bubblegum & Chocolate; lengthen the Trick or Treat table runner by adding logs and squares plus an additional block; and with Lavender Blossoms, add or remove border side or end rail units to change the project size.

Autumn Leaves & Pumpkins, page 162

Bubblegum & Chocolate Patchwork, page 12

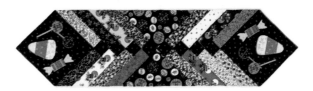

Trick or Treat Runner, page 167

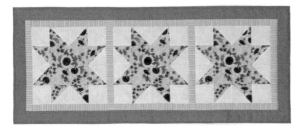

Fussy-Cut Floral Stars, page 23

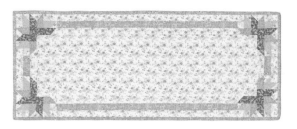

Lavender Blossoms, page 20

• Are the block or border elements suitable for use as half or partial blocks, or must they only be used whole? Most pieced borders can only be expanded in regular units, sometimes exclusively as odd or even repeats.

• Can you enlarge or reduce the blocks, either by simple drafting-size changes or through photocopying to achieve the new size? One way to increase the width of the Floating Blossoms runner from approximately 11" to approximately 15" would be to photocopy the design at 157–160 percent. To lengthen Roses & Rosebuds, photocopy the rosebud paper-pieced border unit enlarged from 2" to 2¼" (112–113 percent) to increase the length by 5" overall. Redesign the vine track by photocopying in the same way. Remember to enlarge all other pieces to the larger size.

Floating Blossoms, page 114

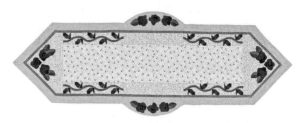

Roses & Rosebuds Runner, page 60

• Are there spaces such as setting strips between the runner center-panel block and other blocks or borders that can be expanded in small or intermediate increments? With the Vintage Hearts & Crazy Patches runner, the size can be easily increased by expanding the center square (with fan blocks moving away from the center crazy square). Adjustments would be needed for repeats within the borders.

Vintage Hearts & Crazy Patches, page 124

• Can a new element or section be added at the center of the runner to reach the desired length?

• Would a new end shape increase the length, either by being made into a point, or by removing the point to form a blunt or squared end? For the Cookout Table Runner, pointed ends could be fashioned from a diagonal half of the center checkerboard.

Cookout Table Runner, page 156

Changing Width

Width changes for a runner project are often less dramatic than those for length. The simplest solutions for enlarging will involve widening background spaces or border, or adding an extra border or two at runner edges. Here are some other solutions to consider:

• When significant width increase is needed, design a pieced border that will repeat an element shape from the interior patchwork. Take care to consider how any original pieced or appliquéd side or end borders or panels are affected by width changes. Reconfigure these for the new layout as needed. Take a look at Chasing the Bear and Reindeer in the Pines runner designs to see how pieced borders can enhance a center panel.

Chasing the Bear, page 30

Reindeer in the Pines, page 66

• If the pattern allows, add a strip with a simple wavy bias vine and appliquéd leaves along both sides of the runner center. Simple appliqué is often a very good complement to geometric shapes.

• If center blocks are a smaller scale, add another row to easily increase the width. Check that added or existing borders stay in proportion.

• Rotate straight-set blocks to be on-point to increase center-panel width by 40 percent. Fill in the edges with plain triangles and add an interesting quilting design in the new space. Similarly, rotate on-point blocks to a straight set. A change from on-point to straight-set would work to narrow the width of Elegant Blue Iris.

Elegant Blue Iris, page 55

Find Element Sizes Within the Pattern

Carefully read project instructions and patterns to determine the finished-block sizes, border widths and lengths, or isolated shape sizes that create the original layout. Use these to make a plan for your changes. Since these are most often listed as cut sizes, subtract the ¼" from each cut edge. In some instances, you will need to re-create the block layout by photocopying templates as provided, cutting out shapes without seams, and then reassembling them on graph paper with a glue stick. Once this is done you can more easily take measurements and consider redesign possibilities.

Create a New Draft Layout

If the original layout or the planned changes are simple, this may be a quick pencil drawing on plain or graph paper, not necessarily to scale. Sketch the blocks and spaces in their general relationship, add notes about new block sizes, new spacer strips, fabric or color selections, etc. Use a calculator to add the various measurements that will compose the length to figure borders, etc. Experiment with size changes, either by multiplying main blocks or changing spacer strip widths until target length is achieved.

If the changes will be more complex and specific, it may be helpful to prepare a true-scale draft on graph paper. An essential tool for construction, a draft will also help you visualize the final design to check that pleasing proportions are preserved. Draw your penciled draft in half-scale (where the ¼" graph paper cell equals ½") or quarter-scale (¼" cell equals 1"). You can add lines on paper to indicate block, setting strip and border elements, and size notes, but leave out patchwork and appliqué detail. To help make experimental arrangement and changes easier, cut small graph-paper blocks that can be moved around, taped or traced in place.

Finalize Your Plan

Once you have finished experimenting, select the best solution. If several solutions seem feasible, photocopy one mock-up to compare before rearranging for a second or third. Clearly ink in size notations, then make sure to add ¼" seam allowances on all sides of new border strips, patches, template shapes, etc. Mark these in red ink to make them readily identifiable. Finally, proceed with the cutting and stitching.

Working With Appliqué Layouts

If appliqué elements are a feature, use exact-size photocopies of the original layout to cut up and rearrange. Add whole or partial motifs to enlarge, or take away portions to reduce or simplify. Begin by sketching the boundaries of the modified design area that you have taken from the original design. Move cutouts around until a pleasing arrangement is achieved, then tape or glue in place. When appliquéd vines are included in a layout, a flexible-curve tool may help establish the new vine placement. Cutting and spreading the vine in strategic locations is another effective method.

Estimating New Yardage Requirements

With final changes decided upon, figure the new fabric amounts you will need. Follow the guidelines that apply to your specific redesign.

• If simple measurement adjustments were made, it is possible that the original yardage will be adequate for both plain or pieced borders.

• If narrow plain borders were added, ballpark an estimate of additional yardage you will need. Half-inch plain borders will require ⅛ yard or slightly more; 1"–2" plain borders will require ¼ yard more. Pieced borders may require ⅛ yard more per fabric added.

• Follow these steps for a more precise yardage plan:

1. List the fabrics used in the new blocks or pieced borders.

2. List each cut shape for the size and quantity needed.

3. Figure how many of each shape can be cut across the fabric width.

4. Divide 42" fabric width by side-to-side patch or shape size. For instance, if cutting 2½" squares, 42" fabric width divided by 2½" (patch width) equals 16.8 or 16 complete squares that can be cut across the fabric width.

5. Figure how many fabric-width strips will be needed to yield the required patches. For example, if 50 of the 2½" squares are needed, 50 divided by 16 squares per strip equals 3.125, rounded up to the next full number equals four strips. Four 2½"-wide strips equal 10" in yardage.

6. Repeat the process for each patch on each fabric list. Combine yardage for shapes from common fabric to determine the total yardage in inches then convert to customary cutting increments—¼, ⅜ or ½ yard, etc.

7. When figuring rectangles, be sure to use appropriate cut width and length of patch. You can pair up triangles into a square to more easily figure how many fit across the yardage, but remember that each square yields two triangles. Similarly, square-up odd shapes into more manageable squares or rectangles.

Whether you choose to make a runner just like the original version given in this book, or you choose to make design changes, you have many designs from which to choose and something for almost any occasion. ◈

Patchwork Only

If your favorite technique is piecing, take an extra-long look at the runners in this chapter. Whether you are a beginning quilter or an accomplished quilter, these pleasing patchwork runners reign supreme.

Bubblegum & Chocolate Patchwork

Design by Julie Weaver

Bubblegum pink and chocolate brown, popular in the 70s, made a huge comeback in recent years.

Project Specifications
Skill Level: Beginner
Runner Size: 41" x 17"

Materials
- 23—3¼" x 3¼" scrap B squares pink, burgundy and brown prints
- ⅓ yard pink print
- ½ yard cream/pink print
- ⅔ yard brown print
- Batting 47" x 23"
- Backing 47" x 23"
- Neutral-color all-purpose thread
- Quilting thread
- Basic sewing tools and supplies

Cutting
1. Cut two 3¼" by fabric width strips cream/pink print; subcut strips into (23) 3¼" A squares.

2. Cut three 2½" by fabric width strips cream/pink print; subcut strips into eight 10½" C strips.

3. Cut three 1½" by fabric width strips pink print; subcut strips into two 34½" D strips and two 12½" E strips.

4. Cut three 1½" by fabric width strips brown print; subcut strips into two 36½" F strips and two 14½" G strips.

5. Cut three 1" by fabric width strips pink print; subcut strips into two 38½" H strips and two 15½" I strips.

6. Cut three 1½" by fabric width strips brown print; subcut strips into two 39½" J strips and two 17½" K strips.

7. Cut four 2¼" by fabric width strips brown print for binding.

Completing the Hourglass Units
1. Draw a diagonal line from corner to corner on the wrong side of each B square.

2. Place a B square right sides together with an A square and stitch ¼" on each side of the marked line as shown in Figure 1.

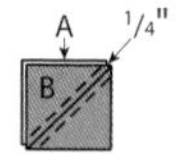

Figure 1

3. Cut apart on the marked line to make two A-B squares as shown in Figure 2; press seam toward B.

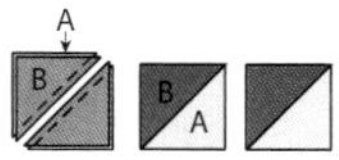

Figure 2

4. Draw a diagonal line across the previously stitched seam on the back side of one of the A-B squares as shown in Figure 3; place this marked square right sides together with the second A-B square aligning A with B, again referring to Figure 3. Sew ¼" on each side of the marked line as shown in Figure 4.

Figure 3   **Figure 4**

5. Cut the stitched unit apart on the marked line to make two A-B units as shown in Figure 5.

Figure 5

6. Repeat steps 2–5 to complete 46 A-B units (discard 1).

Completing the Top

1. Join five A-B units as shown in Figure 6 to make an A row. Press seams toward B sides. Repeat to make four A rows.

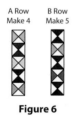

A Row
Make 4   B Row
Make 5

Figure 6

2. Join five A-B units to make a B row, again referring to Figure 6. Press seams to the B sides. Repeat to make five B rows.

3. Arrange and join the A and B rows with C strips to complete the pieced center, referring to the Placement Diagram for positioning; press seams toward C strips.

4. Sew D strips to long sides and E strips to short ends of the pieced center; press seams toward D and E strips.

5. Continue adding strips to long sides and short ends in alphabetical order, pressing seams toward darker strips after each strip is added to complete the pieced top.

Completing the Runner

1. Sandwich the batting between the completed top and prepared backing; pin or baste layers together to hold.

2. Quilt as desired by hand or machine; remove pins or basting. Trim excess backing and batting even with runner top.

3. Join binding strips on short ends to make one long strip; press seams open. Fold the strip in half along length with wrong sides together; press.

4. Sew binding to the right side of the runner edges, mitering corners and overlapping ends. Fold binding to the back side and stitch in place to finish. ◈

Bubblegum & Chocolate Patchwork
Placement Diagram 41" x 17"

Stepping Stones

Design by Julie Weaver

Using a simple piecing method makes this runner quick and easy to complete.

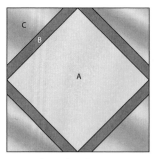

Stepping Stones
10" x 10" Block
Make 4

Project Specifications
Skill Level: Beginner
Runner Size: 48" x 18"
Block Size: 10" x 10"
Number of Blocks: 4

Materials
- ½ yard cream tonal
- ⅔ yard cream floral
- 1¼ yards green tonal *black*
- Batting 54" x 24"
- Backing 54" x 24"
- Neutral-color all-purpose thread
- Quilting thread
- Basic sewing tools and supplies

Cutting
Note: Fabric must be 43" wide to complete border strips without piecing.

1. Cut one 10½" by fabric width strip cream tonal; subcut strip into four 10½" A squares.

2. Cut three 5½" by fabric width strips green tonal; subcut strips into (16) 5½" B squares and four 3½" x 3½" L squares.

3. Cut three 1½" by fabric width strips green tonal; subcut strips into two 40½" D strips and two 12½" E strips.

4. Cut six 1" by fabric width G/J strips green tonal.

5. Cut four 2¼" by fabric width strips green tonal for binding.

6. Cut six 1" by fabric width F/I strips cream floral. *yellow*

7. Cut three 1½" by fabric width H/K strips cream floral.

8. Cut two 4½" by fabric width strips cream floral; subcut strips into (16) 4½" C squares. *yellow*

Completing the Blocks
1. Draw a diagonal line from corner to corner on the wrong side of each B and C square.

2. Place a C square right sides together on one corner of one B square; stitch on the marked line as shown in Figure 1.

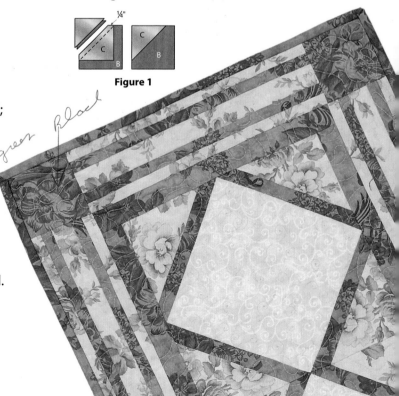

Figure 1

3. Trim seam to ¼" and press C to the right side to complete a B-C unit, again referring to Figure 1; repeat to make 16 B-C units.

4. To complete one Stepping Stones block, place a B-C unit on one corner of an A square as shown in Figure 2; stitch on the marked line. Trim seam to ¼" and press the B-C unit to the right side, again referring to Figure 2.

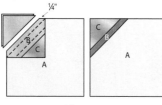

Figure 2

5. Repeat step 4 on each corner of A to complete one block; repeat to make four blocks.

Completing the Top

1. Join the four blocks to complete the pieced center; press seams in one direction.

2. Sew D strips to opposite long sides and E strips to opposite short ends of the pieced center; press seams toward D and E strips.

3. Join two each F/I and G/J strips with H/K with right sides together along length to make a strip set as shown in Figure 3; press seams toward G/J. Repeat to make three strip sets. Trim two strip sets to 42½" for F-G-H; cut two 12½" I-J-K strips from the remaining strip set.

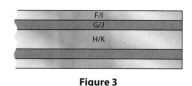

Figure 3

4. Sew an F-G-H strip to opposite long sides of the pieced center; press seams toward D strips.

5. Sew an L square to each end of each I-J-K strip to make an end strip as shown in Figure 4; press seams toward L.

Figure 4

6. Sew an end strip to opposite short ends of the pieced center to complete the pieced top.

Completing the Runner

1. Sandwich the batting between the completed top and prepared backing; pin or baste layers together.

2. Quilt as desired by hand or machine; remove pins or basting. Trim excess backing and batting even with runner top.

3. Join binding strips on short ends to make one long strip; press seams open. Fold the strip in half along length with wrong sides together; press.

4. Sew binding to the right side of the runner edges, mitering corners and overlapping ends. Fold binding to the back side and stitch in place to finish. ◈

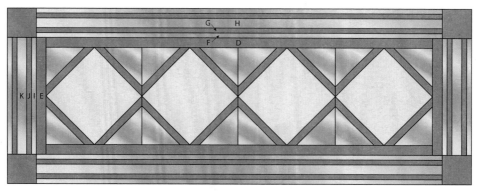

Stepping Stones
Placement Diagram 48" x 18"

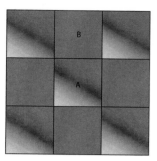

Nine-Patch
9" x 9" Block
Make 3

Blocks 'n' Buttons

Design by Nancy Richoux

Buttons connect the blocks
in this simple pieced runner.

Project Specifications
Skill Level: Beginner
Runner Size: 39¼" x 12¾"
Block Size: 9" x 9"
Number of Blocks: 3

Materials
- 1 fat quarter each dark floral and light rose tonal
- ⅞ yard dark rose tonal
- 5 (13" x 13") batting squares
- White and neutral-color all-purpose thread
- Quilting thread
- 40 (¾") white buttons
- Basic sewing tools and supplies

Cutting
1. Cut three 3½" x 21" A strips dark floral.

2. Cut two 3½" by fabric width B strips dark rose tonal; cut strips in half to make four 21" strips.

3. Cut five 13" x 13" backing squares dark rose tonal.

4. Cut two 9½" x 9½" C squares light rose tonal.

Completing the Blocks
1. Sew a B strip between two A strips to make an A-B strip set; press seams open.

2. Subcut the A-B strip set into six 3½" A-B rows as shown in Figure 1.

3. Sew an A strip between two B strips to make a B-A strip set; press seams open.

4. Subcut the B-A strip set into three 3½" B-A rows as shown in Figure 2.

5. Sew a B-A row between two A-B rows to complete one Nine-Patch block referring to the block drawing; press seams open. Repeat to complete three Nine-Patch blocks.

Completing the Runner
1. Sandwich one square of batting between one backing square and a completed Nine-Patch block, centering the block on the batting/backing layers; quilt as desired by hand or machine.

2. Trim edges of batting only even with edges of the Nine-Patch block. Trim backing to ⅝" beyond edges of block/batting layers.

3. Fold under the edges of the backing ¼" all around and press.

4. Fold the backing to the block side of the quilted unit as shown in Figure 3; hand-stitch in place, mitering corners.

Figure 3

Figure 1   **Figure 2**

5. Repeat steps 1–4 with remaining Nine-Patch blocks and C squares to complete three quilted block squares and two quilted C squares.

6. Overlap quilted Nine-Patch blocks on C squares with seams between A and B squares aligned with edge of C as shown in Figure 4; pin to hold.

7. Referring to the Placement Diagram, evenly space and stitch four buttons in the exposed corners of C squares and in the overlapped A squares, stitching through the C squares to connect quilted units and complete the runner. ◈

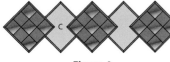

Figure 4

Blocks 'n' Buttons
Placement Diagram 39¼" x 12¾"

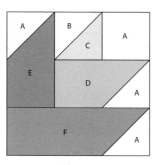

Flower
3" x 3" Block
Make 12

Lavender Blossoms

Design by Julie Weaver

Blocks accent the corners of this open-center romantic-looking runner.

Project Specifications
Skill Level: Beginner
Runner Size: 39" x 15"
Block Size: 3" x 3"
Number of Blocks: 12

Materials
- ⅛ yard pale lavender print
- ⅛ yard light lavender print
- ⅛ yard medium lavender print
- ⅛ yard dark lavender print
- ⅜ yard green print
- ⅔ yard cream print
- Batting 45" x 21"
- Backing 45" x 21"
- Neutral-color all-purpose thread
- Quilting thread
- Basic sewing tools and supplies

Cutting
1. Cut two 1½" by fabric width strips cream print; subcut strips into (48) 1½" A squares.

2. Cut one 1⅞" by fabric width strip cream print; subcut strip into six 1⅞" squares. Cut each square in half on one diagonal to make 12 B triangles.

3. Cut one 9½" x 33½" G rectangle cream print.

4. Cut four 1½" by fabric width H strips cream print.

5. Cut one 1⅞" by fabric width strip pale lavender print; subcut strip into six 1⅞" squares. Cut each square in half on one diagonal to make 12 C triangles.

6. Cut one 1½" by fabric width strip light lavender print; subcut strip into (12) 2½" D pieces.

7. Cut one 1½" by fabric width strip medium lavender print; subcut strip into (12) 2½" E pieces.

8. Cut one 1½" by fabric width strip dark lavender print; subcut strip into (12) 3½" F pieces.

9. Cut two 1½" by fabric width I strips green print.

10. Cut three 2¼" by fabric width strips green print for binding.

Completing the Blocks
1. Set aside 12 A squares; mark a diagonal line from corner to corner on the wrong side of each remaining A square.

2. Place an A square right sides together on one end of D and stitch on the marked line as shown in Figure 1; trim to make a ¼" seam allowance and press A to the right side to complete an A-D unit, again referring to Figure 1. Repeat to make 12 A-D units.

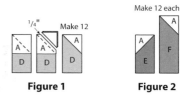

Figure 1   **Figure 2**

3. Repeat step 2 with A and E to make 12 A-E units and with A and F to make 12 A-F units as shown in Figure 2.

4. Sew B to C to complete a B-C unit as shown in Figure 3; press seam toward C. Repeat to make 12 B-C units.

Figure 3   **Figure 4**

5. To complete one Flower block, sew A to a B-C unit as shown in Figure 4; press seam toward A.

6. Add an A-D unit to the A-B-C unit as shown in Figure 5; press seam toward the A-D unit.

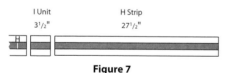

Figure 5   **Figure 6**

7. Add an A-E unit and then an A-F unit to the stitched unit to complete one block referring to Figure 6; press seam toward A-E and then A-F.

8. Repeat steps 5–7 to complete 12 Flower blocks.

Completing the Top

1. Sew an I strip between two H strips with right sides together along length; press seams toward the I strip. Repeat to make two H-I strip sets.

2. Subcut each H-I strip set into one each 27½" H strip and 3½" I unit as shown in Figure 7.

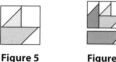

Figure 7

3. Sew a Flower block to each end of each H strip as shown in Figure 8; press seams toward H strip.

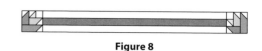

Figure 8

4. Sew the Flower/H-I strip to opposite sides of G; press seams toward G.

5. Join two Flower blocks as shown in Figure 9; press seam in one direction. Repeat to make four two-block units.

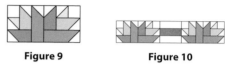

Figure 9   **Figure 10**

6. Sew a two-block unit to opposite ends of each I unit to make end units as shown in Figure 10; press seams toward I units.

7. Sew an end unit to each end of the stitched G unit to complete the pieced center, referring to the Placement Diagram for positioning.

Completing the Runner

1. Sandwich the batting between the completed top and prepared backing; pin or baste layers together to hold.

2. Quilt as desired by hand or machine; remove pins or basting. Trim excess backing and batting even with runner top.

3. Join binding strips on short ends to make one long strip; press seams open. Fold the strip in half along length with wrong sides together; press.

4. Sew binding to the right side of the runner edges, mitering corners and overlapping ends. Fold binding to the back side and stitch in place to finish. ◈

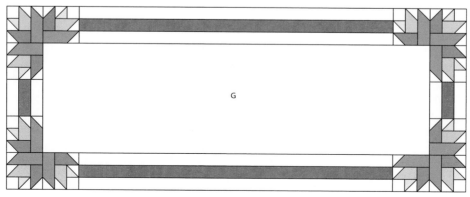

Lavender Blossoms
Placement Diagram 39" x 15"

Fussy-Cut Floral Stars

Design by Nancy Richoux

A bright-colored sunflower print brightens
the star blocks in this pretty runner.

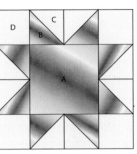

Star
12" x 12" Block
Make 3

Project Specifications
Skill Level: Beginner
Runner Size: 44" x 18"
Block Size: 12" x 12"
Number of Blocks: 3

Materials
- ¼ yard blue tonal stripe
- ½ yard yellow tonal
- ⅝ yard blue tonal
- ¾ yard floral print with 3 repeats of floral motif to fit 6½" square
- Batting 50" x 24"
- Backing 50" x 24"
- Neutral-color all-purpose thread
- Quilting thread
- Basic sewing tools and supplies

Cutting
1. Cut three 6" x 6" A squares floral print, centering a motif in each square.

2. Cut two 3⅞" by fabric width strips floral print; subcut strips into (12) 3⅞" squares. Cut each square in half on one diagonal to make 24 B triangles.

3. Cut two 3⅞" by fabric width strips yellow tonal; subcut strips into (12) 3⅞" squares. Cut each square in half on one diagonal to make 24 C triangles.

4. Cut one 3½" by fabric width strip yellow tonal; subcut strips into (12) 3½" D squares.

5. Cut four 1½" by fabric width strips blue tonal stripe; subcut strips into six 12½" E strips and four 14½" F strips.

6. Cut two 2½" x 40½" G strips and two 2½" x 18½" H strips blue tonal.

7. Cut four 2¼" by fabric width strips blue tonal for binding.

Completing the Star Blocks

1. Sew a C triangle to a B triangle along the diagonal to make a B-C unit as shown in Figure 1; press seams toward B. Repeat to make 24 B-C units.

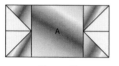

Figure 1   **Figure 2**

2. To complete one Star block, join two B-C units to make a side unit as shown in Figure 2; press seam in one direction. Repeat to make four side units.

3. Sew a side unit to opposite sides of A to complete the center row as shown in Figure 3; press seams toward A.

Figure 3   **Figure 4**

4. Sew D to each end of each remaining side unit to make a row as shown in Figure 4; press seams toward D. Repeat to make two rows.

5. Sew the rows to opposite long sides of the center row to complete one block referring to the block drawing for positioning of rows; press seams toward the center row.

6. Repeat steps 2–5 to complete three Star blocks.

Completing the Top

1. Sew an E strip to two opposite sides of each Star block; press seams toward E.

> *When centering motifs in shapes, draw out the size of the shape on paper or card stock; cut out the shape to make a "window" to place over fabric to help with selecting and cutting the design to fit within the shape perfectly.*
>
> *~Nancy Richoux*

2. Join the E-bordered Star blocks with F strips; press seams toward F.

3. Sew G strips to the long sides and H strips to the short ends of the pieced center to complete the pieced top; press seams toward G and H strips.

Completing the Runner

1. Sandwich the batting between the completed top and prepared backing; pin or baste layers together to hold.

2. Quilt as desired by hand or machine; remove pins or basting. Trim excess backing and batting even with runner top.

3. Join binding strips on short ends to make one long strip; press seams open. Fold the strip in half along length with wrong sides together; press.

4. Sew binding to the right side of the runner edges, mitering corners and overlapping ends. Fold binding to the back side and stitch in place to finish. ◈

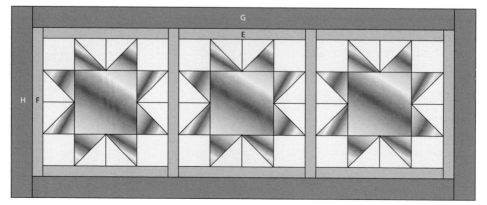

Fussy-Cut Floral Stars
Placement Diagram 44" x 18"

Star Points Runner

Design by Sandra L. Hatch

An old-fashioned six-pointed star design in two colors makes a striking runner.

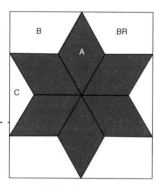

Six-Pointed Star
14" x 16" Block
Make 2

Project Specifications
Skill Level: Intermediate
Runner Size: 56" x 16"
Block Size: 14" x 16"
Number of Blocks: 2

Materials
- ⅔ yard red print
- ⅔ yard white tonal
- Batting 59" x 19"
- Backing 59" x 19"
- All-purpose thread to match fabrics
- Quilting thread
- Basic sewing tools and supplies

Cutting
1. Prepare templates for pieces A–C using patterns given; cut as directed on each piece. Place a dot at the junction of all seam allowances for precision piecing.

Completing the Six-Pointed Star Blocks
1. Join three A pieces, stopping stitching at the end of the marked seam allowances as shown in Figure 1; press seams to one side. Repeat to make two joined A units.

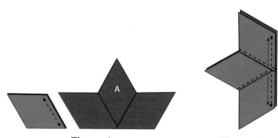

Figure 1   **Figure 2**

2. Join the two A units, starting seams at the marked center point and stitching toward the outside, stopping stitching at the marked dots, to complete the star unit as shown in Figure 2.

3. Sew in B and C pieces, matching marked points and pivoting stitching at the angled seam junctions as shown in Figure 3 to complete one Six-Pointed Star block.

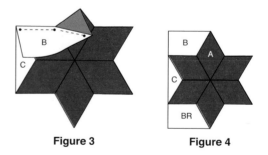

Figure 3   **Figure 4**

4. Repeat steps 1–3 to complete two Six-Pointed Star blocks.

5. Repeat steps 1–3 to complete two partial six-pointed star units as shown in Figure 4.

Completing the Top

1. Join the two Six-Pointed Star blocks and add a partial unit to each end referring to the Placement Diagram to complete the pieced top.

Completing the Runner

1. Place backing piece right side up on batting; place completed top right sides together with backing; pin edges.

2. Trim backing and batting even with the pieced top.

3. Sew all around, leaving a 4" opening along one side; clip inner corners. Trim batting close to stitching.

4. Turn right side out through opening; press edges flat.

5. Turn opening edges to the inside; hand-stitch opening closed.

6. Quilt as desired by hand or machine to finish. ◈

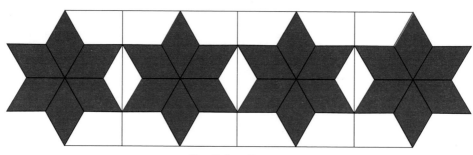

Star Points Runner
Placement Diagram 56" x 16"

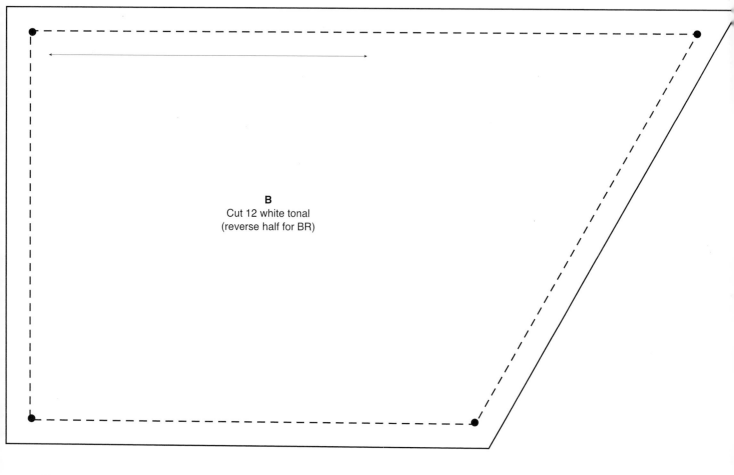

B
Cut 12 white tonal
(reverse half for BR)

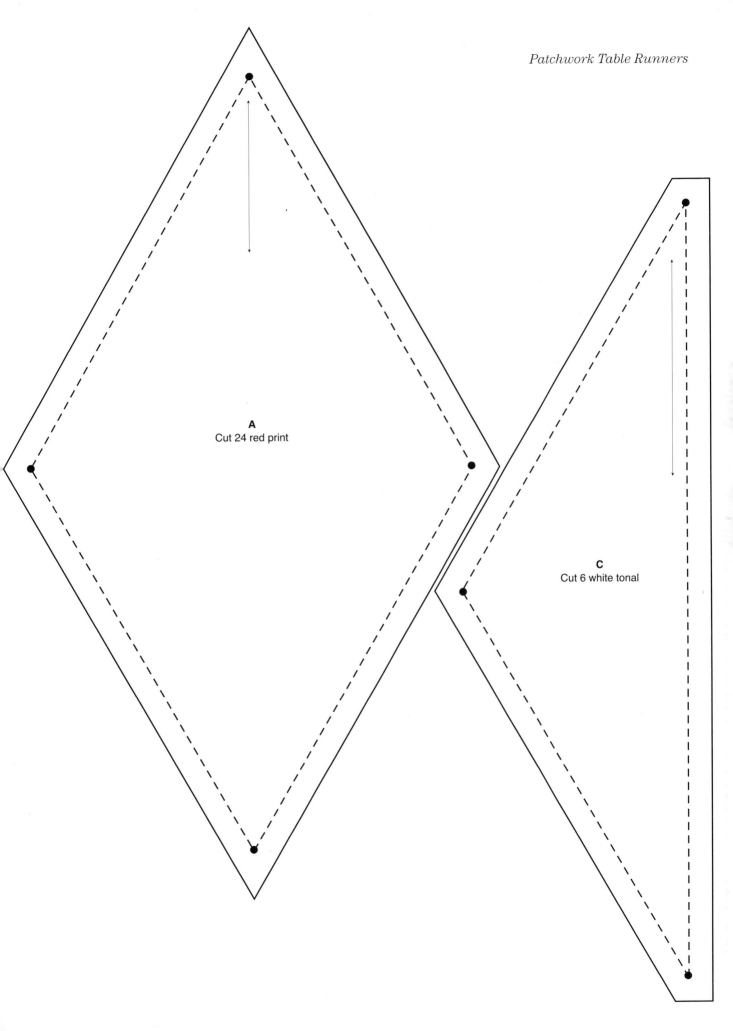

A
Cut 24 red print

C
Cut 6 white tonal

Chasing the Bear

Design by Julie Weaver

Combine scrap fabrics in autumn colors to create a beautiful table cover.

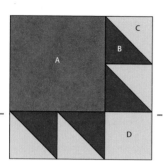

Paw
4½" x 4½" Block
Make 16

Project Notes

I chose five fabrics each from different gold, green, orange, red and brown prints—anything that reminded me of fall colors. By using the same background throughout, I controlled the scrappy look of the project. However, this runner could be a true scrap quilt by using a wide variety of fall-colored prints and background prints—a great stash buster.

Project Specifications

Skill Level: Beginner
Runner Size: 50" x 20"
Block Size: 4½" x 4½"
Number of Blocks: 16

Materials

- ⅛ yard each or scraps 5 different red, orange, brown, green and gold prints, mottleds or tonals
- ⅛ yard medium brown tonal
- ½ yard dark brown mottled
- 1 yard cream print
- Batting 56" x 26"
- Backing 56" x 26"
- Neutral-color all-purpose thread
- Quilting thread
- Basic sewing tools and supplies

Cutting

1. Cut (16) 3½" x 3½" A squares total from the five different red, orange, brown, green and gold fabrics.

2. Cut 16 matching pairs total 2⅜" x 2⅜" B squares from the five different red, orange, brown, green and gold fabrics. ***Note:*** *Two matching squares will form the claws on one Paw block.*

3. Cut a total of (62) 2½" x 4½" J rectangles from the five different red, orange, brown, green and gold fabrics.

4. Cut two 2⅜" by fabric width strips cream print; subcut strips into (32) 2⅜" C squares.

5. Cut one 2" by fabric width strip cream print; subcut strip into (16) 2" D squares.

6. Cut eight 2½" by fabric width strips cream print; subcut strips into (124) 2½" K squares.

7. Cut four 1½" by fabric width strips dark brown mottled; subcut one strip into three 9½" E strips. From the remaining strips, cut two 39½" F strips and two 11½" G strips.

8. Cut four 2¼" by fabric width strips dark brown mottled for binding.

9. Cut three 1" by fabric width strips brown tonal; subcut strips into two 41½" H strips and two 12½" I strips.

Completing the Blocks

1. Draw a diagonal line from corner to corner on the wrong side of each C square.

2. Place a C square right sides together with a B square; stitch ¼" on each side of the marked line as shown in Figure 1.

Figure 1

3. Cut apart on the marked line and press open with seam toward B to complete two B-C units, again referring to Figure 1. Repeat with all B and C squares to complete 64 B-C units.

4. To complete one Paw block, select four matching B-C units. Join two B-C units as shown in Figure 2; repeat. Press seams in one direction.

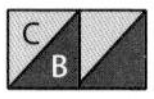

Figure 2

5. Sew a B-C row to one side of A as shown in Figure 3; press seam toward A.

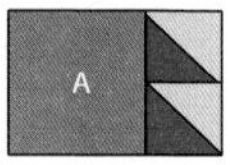

Figure 3

6. Sew D to one end of the remaining stitched B-C row as shown in Figure 4; press seam toward D.

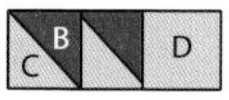

Figure 4

7. Sew the B-C-D unit to the stitched A unit to complete one Paw block as shown in Figure 5; press seam toward the A unit.

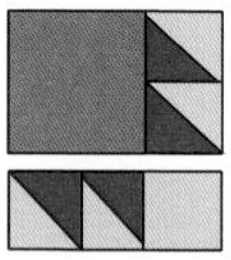

Figure 5

8. Repeat steps 4–7 to complete 16 Paw blocks.

Completing the Top

1. Join two Paw blocks to make a row as shown in Figure 6; press seam in one direction. Repeat to make two rows.

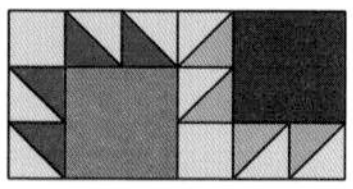

Figure 6

2. Join the rows referring to the Placement Diagram to complete a four-block unit; press seam in one direction. Repeat to make four four-block units.

3. Join the four-block units with the three E strips to complete the pieced center; press seams toward E strips.

4. Sew F strips to opposite long sides and G strips to opposite short ends of the pieced center; press seams toward F and G strips.

5. Sew H strips to opposite long sides and I strips to opposite short ends of the pieced center; press seams toward H and I strips.

6. Draw a diagonal line from corner to corner on the wrong side of each K square.

7. Place a K square on one end of J and stitch on the marked line as shown in Figure 7; trim seam to ¼" and press K to the right side, again referring to Figure 7.

Figure 7

8. Repeat step 7 with K on the remaining end of J to complete a J-K unit as shown in Figure 8. Repeat to make 62 J-K units.

Figure 8

9. Join 21 J-K units to make a side strip as shown in Figure 9; press seams in one direction. Repeat to make two side strips.

Figure 9

10. Sew a side strip to opposite sides of the pieced center referring to the Placement Diagram for positioning; press seams away from the side strips. ***Note:*** *Strips reverse direction on the sample quilt.*

11. Join eight J-K units as in step 8; press seams in one direction. Repeat to make two eight-unit strips.

12. Join two J-K units; press seam to one side. Repeat to make two two-unit strips.

13. Sew a two-unit strip to an eight-unit strip to complete an end strip as shown in Figure 10; press seam in one direction. Repeat to make two end strips.

Figure 10

14. Sew an end strip to opposite short ends of the pieced center to complete the pieced top; press seams away from end strips.

Completing the Runner

1. Sandwich the batting between the completed top and prepared backing; pin or baste layers together.

2. Quilt as desired by hand or machine; remove pins or basting. Trim excess backing and batting even with runner top.

3. Join binding strips on short ends to make one long strip; press seams open. Fold the strip in half along length with wrong sides together; press.

4. Sew binding to the right side of the runner edges, mitering corners and overlapping ends. Fold binding to the back side and stitch in place to finish. ◈

Chasing the Bear
Placement Diagram 50" x 20"

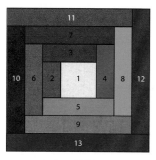

Log Cabin
12" x 12" Block
Make 6

Christmas Logs

Design by Sandra L. Hatch

Use Christmas scraps for an easy runner.

Project Specifications
Skill Level: Beginner
Runner Size: 58" x 24"
Block Size: 12" x 12"
Number of Blocks: 6

Materials
- Scraps red, green and cream Christmas prints
- 1/3 yard red metallic print
- 1/2 yard green metallic print
- Batting 64" x 30"
- Backing 64" x 30"
- Neutral-color all-purpose thread
- Gold metallic thread
- Quilting thread
- Basic sewing tools and supplies

Cutting
1. From red scraps, cut six 2"-wide pieces in each of the following lengths: piece 2–3½"; piece 3–5"; piece 6–6½"; piece 7–8"; piece 10– 9½"; and piece 11–11".

2. From green scraps, cut six 2"-wide pieces in each of the following lengths: piece 4–5"; piece 5–6½"; piece 8–8"; piece 9–9½"; piece 12–11" and piece 13–12½".

3. Cut six 3½" x 3½" squares cream scrap for piece 1.

4. Prepare template for X using pattern given; cut as directed.

5. Cut three 2¼" by fabric width strips red metallic print for binding.

Completing the Blocks
1. Select one piece 1 square and one piece 2 strip; sew piece 2 to piece 1 as shown in Figure 1. Press seam toward piece 2. Continue to add strips in numerical order through piece 13 to complete one Log Cabin block referring to Block diagram for number sequence; press seams toward most recently added strip before adding another strip.

Figure 1

2. Repeat step 1 to complete six Log Cabin blocks.

Completing the Top
1. Join two Log Cabin blocks to make a row as shown in Figure 2; press seam in one direction. Repeat to make two rows.

Figure 2   **Figure 3**

2. Join the two rows to complete the pieced center referring to the Placement Diagram for positioning; press seam in one direction.

3. Sew X to two adjacent sides of each remaining Log Cabin block to make the end units as shown in Figure 3; press seams toward X.

4. Sew an end unit to opposite ends of the pieced center to complete the pieced top; press seams toward end units.

Completing the Runner

1. Sandwich the batting between the completed top and prepared backing; pin or baste layers together.

2. Quilt as desired by hand or machine using gold metallic thread; remove pins or basting. Trim excess backing and batting even with runner top.

3. Join binding strips on short ends to make one long strip; press seams open. Fold the strip in half along length with wrong sides together; press.

4. Sew binding to the right side of the runner edges, mitering corners and overlapping ends. Fold binding to the back side and stitch in place to finish. ◈

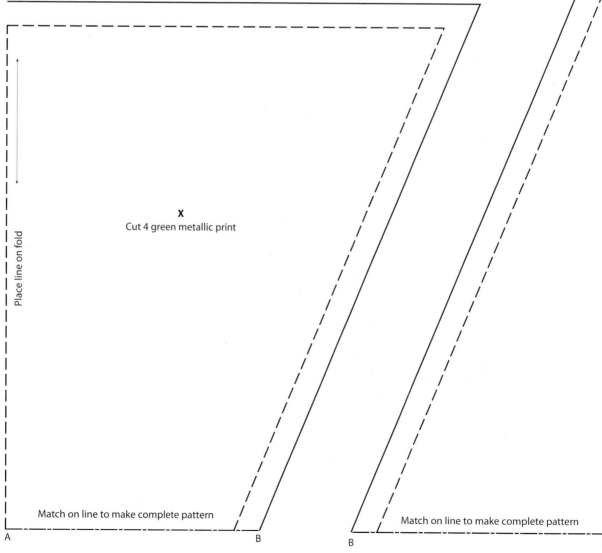

Christmas Logs
Placement Diagram 58" x 24"

Place line on fold

X
Cut 4 green metallic print

Match on line to make complete pattern

Match on line to make complete pattern

A

B

B

A

Add Some Appliqué

If you love to appliqué, you will love the runners in this chapter. They are still patchwork runners, but the added touch of appliqué makes these runners shine like the stars that they are.

Strawberries to Apples

Design by BrendaBarb Designs/Brenda Connelly and Barb Miller

Extend the life of this runner with strawberries for summertime on one side and apples for autumn on the other.

- -

Project Specifications
Skill Level: Beginner
Runner Size: 37½" x 18½"

Materials
- 8–10" x 10 A squares tan tonals and mottleds for apple background
- 8–10" x 10" E squares white tonals and mottleds for strawberry background
- ¼ yard light green mottled
- ¼ yard dark red mottled
- ⅜ yard bright red mottled
- ¾ yard dark green mottled
- Batting 44" x 25"
- Neutral-color all-purpose thread
- Quilting thread
- Invisible thread
- 2 yards lightweight 12"-wide fusible web
- Brown and black fabric pens
- Basic sewing tools and supplies

Cutting
1. Cut (10) 5" x 10" D rectangles from five of the 10" x 10" A squares. Cut (10) 5" x 10" F rectangles from five of the 10" x 10" E squares.

2. Cut four 1" by fabric width strips dark green mottled; subcut into four 10" B strips and four 29" C strips.

3. Cut three 2¼" by fabric width strips dark green mottled for binding.

4. Trace appliqué shapes onto the paper side of the fusible web as directed on patterns for number to cut; cut out shapes leaving a margin around each one.

5. Fuse shapes to the wrong side of fabrics as directed on patterns for color; cut out shapes on traced lines. Remove paper backing.

Completing the Apples Side
1. Join three A squares to complete the runner center; press seams in one direction.

2. Fold and press the B and C strips with wrong sides together along length.

3. Pin and stitch a B strip to opposite short ends of the stitched A center, matching folded raw edges.

4. Repeat step 3 with the C strips on opposite long sides.

5. Join three D rectangles on short ends to make a long D strip; repeat to make two long D strips. Repeat with two D rectangles to make two short D strips. Trim ½" off one end of each short D strip to measure 19" long.

6. Sew a long D strip to opposite long sides and the short D strips to the short ends of the bordered A center; press seams toward the D strips.

Tip

When appliquéing, at the corner of an appliqué piece, put the needle down at the point, turn the fabric one-half position, stitch once, complete turn and continue stitching.

~Barbara Miller
Brenda Connelly

7. Arrange and fuse the apple shapes on the D pieces referring to the patterns and Apples Side Placement Diagram for positioning; repeat with leaf shapes.

8. Using invisible thread and a narrow satin stitch, machine-stitch around each fused shape.

9. Add detail lines to leaves and apples using brown or black fabric pen.

Completing the Strawberries Side

1. Complete the strawberries side using E squares and F rectangles with B and C strips and strawberry appliqué shapes as for Completing the Apples Side and referring to the strawberry patterns and Strawberries Side Placement Diagram for positioning of pieces.

2. Connect the berries with a vine and add details using the brown or black fabric pen.

Completing the Runner

1. Sandwich the batting between the completed tops; pin or baste layers together to hold.

2. Quilt as desired by hand or machine; remove pins or basting. Trim excess backing and batting even with runner top.

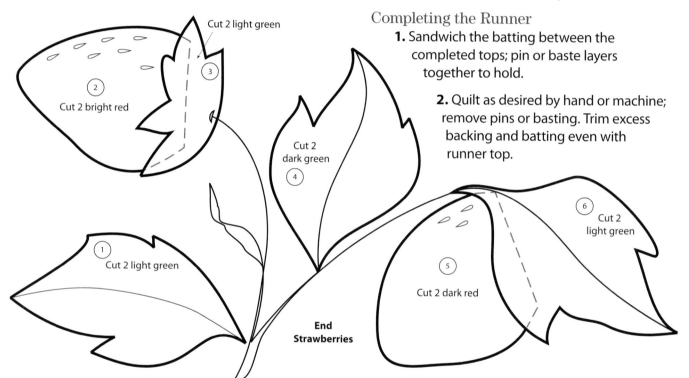

Cut 2 light green

③

② Cut 2 bright red

Cut 2 dark green ④

① Cut 2 light green

End Strawberries

⑥ Cut 2 light green

⑤ Cut 2 dark red

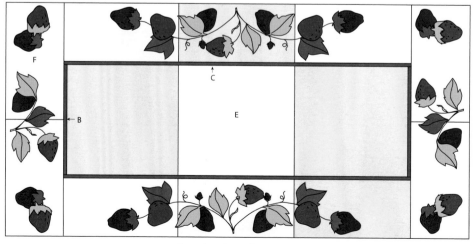

Strawberries Side Runner
Placement Diagram 37½" x 18½"

3. Join binding strips on short ends to make one long strip; press seams open. Fold the strip in half along length with wrong sides together; press.

4. Sew binding to right side of runner edges, mitering corners and overlapping ends. Fold binding to the back side and stitch in place to finish. ◈

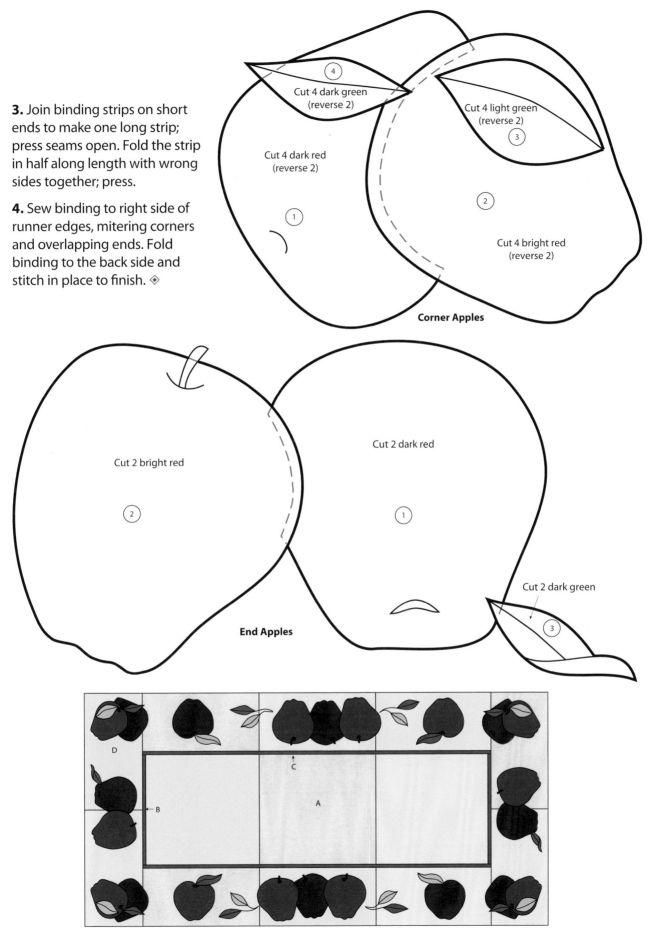

Cut 4 dark green
(reverse 2)
④

Cut 4 light green
(reverse 2)
③

Cut 4 dark red
(reverse 2)
①

②

Cut 4 bright red
(reverse 2)

Corner Apples

Cut 2 bright red
②

Cut 2 dark red
①

End Apples

Cut 2 dark green
③

D

C

B

A

Apples Side Runner
Placement Diagram 37½" x 18½"

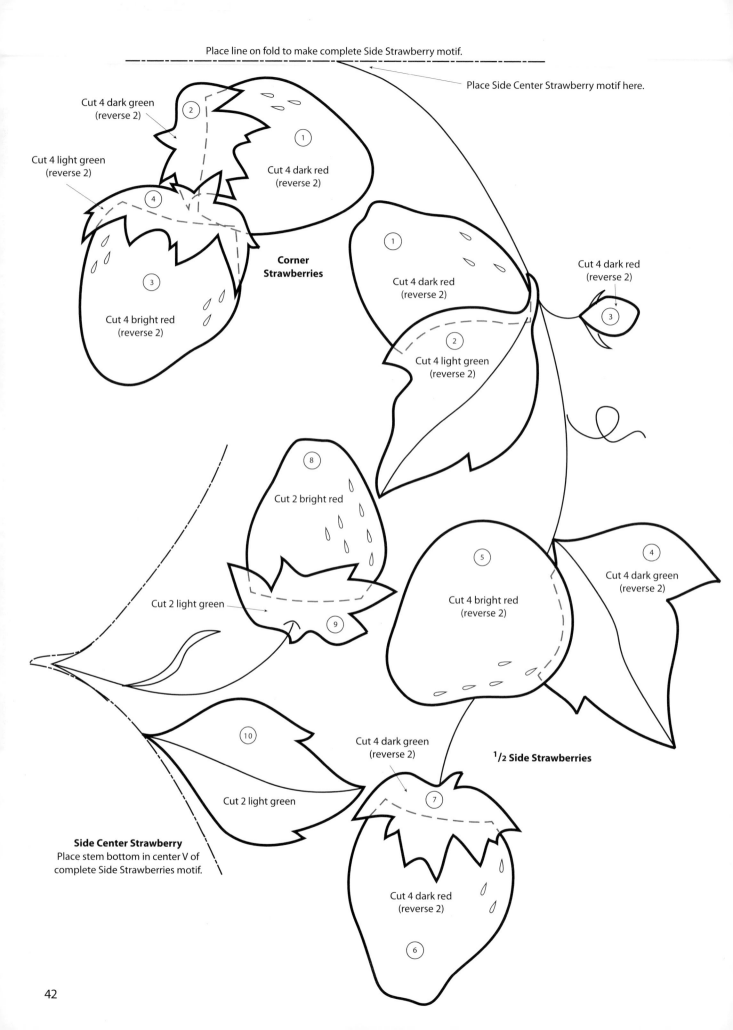

Place line on fold to make complete Side Strawberry motif.

Place Side Center Strawberry motif here.

Cut 4 dark green
(reverse 2)

② ①

Cut 4 light green
(reverse 2)

Cut 4 dark red
(reverse 2)

④ ①

**Corner
Strawberries**

③

Cut 4 bright red
(reverse 2)

Cut 4 dark red
(reverse 2)

② ③

Cut 4 light green
(reverse 2)

⑧

Cut 2 bright red

④

Cut 4 dark green
(reverse 2)

⑤

Cut 4 bright red
(reverse 2)

Cut 2 light green

⑨

⑩

Cut 2 light green

Cut 4 dark green
(reverse 2)

¹/₂ Side Strawberries

⑦

Side Center Strawberry
Place stem bottom in center V of
complete Side Strawberries motif.

Cut 4 dark red
(reverse 2)

⑥

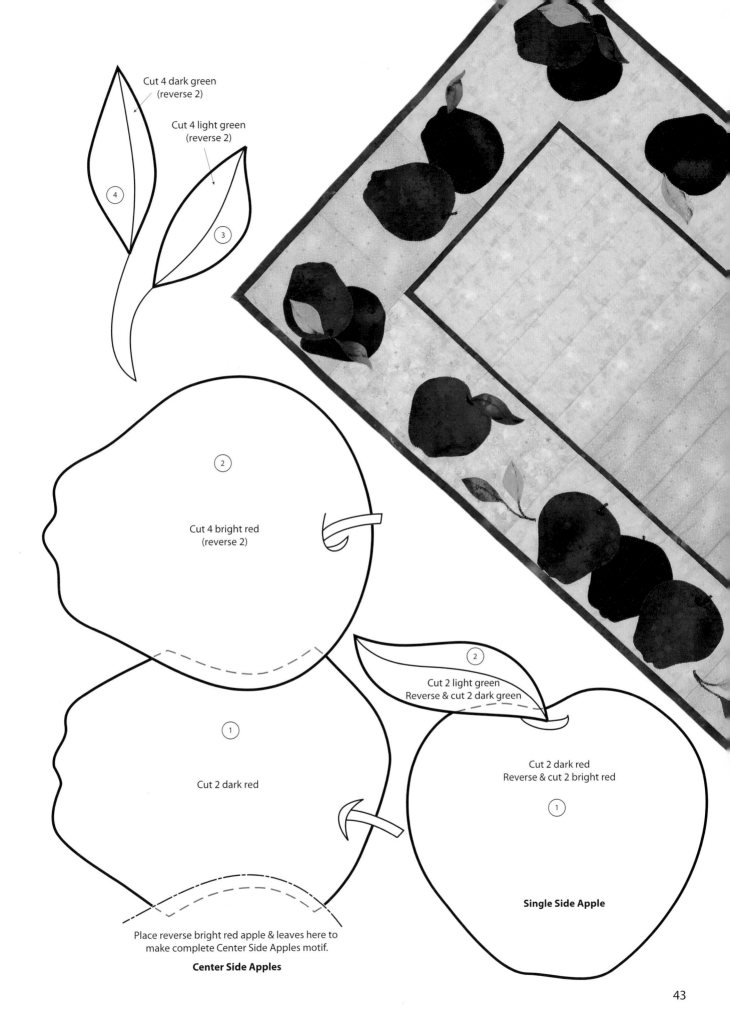

Cut 4 dark green
(reverse 2)

Cut 4 light green
(reverse 2)

④

③

②

Cut 4 bright red
(reverse 2)

②

Cut 2 light green
Reverse & cut 2 dark green

①

Cut 2 dark red

Cut 2 dark red
Reverse & cut 2 bright red

①

Single Side Apple

Place reverse bright red apple & leaves here to
make complete Center Side Apples motif.

Center Side Apples

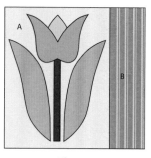

Flower
8" x 8" Block
Make 8

May Flowers

Design by Jill Reber

Appliquéd flowers welcome spring.

Project Specifications
Skill Level: Beginner
Runner Size: 36" x 20"
Block Size: 8" x 8"
Number of Blocks: 8

Materials
- Scraps pink floral, pink and green solids and green/white dot
- ⅓ yard tan floral
- ½ yard cream mottled
- ⅝ yard coordinating stripe
- Batting 42" x 26"
- Backing 42" x 26"
- All-purpose thread to match fabrics
- Quilting thread
- 1 yard 12"-wide fusible web
- ⅞ yard fabric stabilizer
- Basic sewing tools and supplies

Cutting
1. Cut two 6½" by fabric width strips cream mottled; subcut strip into eight 8½" A rectangles.

2. Cut one 8½" by fabric width strip coordinating stripe; subcut strip into eight 2½" B strips.

3. Cut three 2¼" by fabric width strips coordinating stripe for binding.

4. Cut two 2½" x 16½" C strips and two 2½" x 36½" D strips tan floral.

5. Trace appliqué shapes onto the paper side of the fusible web as directed on pattern. Cut out shapes, leaving a margin around each piece.

6. Fuse shapes to the wrong side of fabrics as directed on patterns for color; cut out shapes on traced lines. Remove paper backing.

Completing the Blocks
1. Select one appliqué motif, one A rectangle and one B strip.

2. Fold and crease A along the length to mark the center.

3. Arrange and fuse appliqué pieces on A in numerical order, using center crease as a guide for placement.

4. Sew B to the right side edge of A referring to the block drawing.

5. Repeat steps 1–4 to complete eight fused Flower blocks.

6. Cut eight 6" x 8" pieces fabric stabilizer. Pin a piece behind each fused block.

7. Using thread to match fabrics, machine satin-stitch around shapes to complete the blocks; remove fabric stabilizer.

Completing the Top
1. Arrange and join four blocks to make a row as shown in Figure 1; press seams in one direction. Repeat to make two rows.

Figure 1

2. Join the rows to complete the pieced center; press seam in one direction.

3. Sew a C strip on each short end and D strips to opposite long sides of the pieced center; press seams toward C and D strips.

Completing the Runner

1. Sandwich the batting between the completed top and prepared backing; pin or baste layers together to hold.

2. Quilt as desired by hand or machine; remove pins or basting. Trim excess backing and batting even with runner top.

3. Join binding strips on short ends to make one long strip; press seams open. Fold the strip in half along length with wrong sides together; press.

4. Sew binding to right side of runner edges, mitering corners and overlapping ends. Fold binding to the back side and stitch in place to finish. ◈

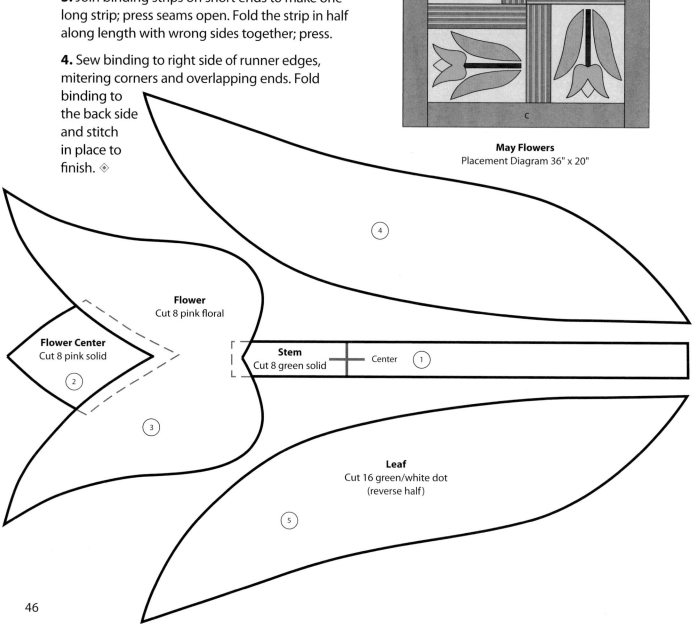

May Flowers
Placement Diagram 36" x 20"

Flower
Cut 8 pink floral

Flower Center
Cut 8 pink solid

Stem
Cut 8 green solid

Center

Leaf
Cut 16 green/white dot
(reverse half)

A Garden Square

Design by Chris Malone

Introduce a bit of summer with 3-D flowers and leaves on this matching runner, napkin and napkin ring set.

Project Notes

Instructions are given to make two napkins and napkin rings. You will need additional fabric, buttons and elastic to make additional napkins and napkin rings—one 17½" square each green print and tan tonal, one button and one strip elastic for each napkin.

Project Specifications

Skill Level: Beginner
Runner Size: 40" x 17½"
Napkin Size: 17" x 17"
Napkin Ring Size: 3¼" x 3½"

Materials

- 6 light–medium green print fat quarters
- 2 light–medium green print fat quarters for napkins
- ¼ yard rose print
- ½ yard green mottled
- 1 yard tan tonal
- Batting 46" x 23"
- Backing 46" x 23"
- Fleece or lightweight batting scraps for appliqués
- All-purpose thread to match fabrics
- Quilting thread
- No-fray solution
- 16 (¾") green short-shank buttons
- 2 (5½") lengths ¾"-wide elastic
- Basic sewing tools and supplies

Cutting

1. Cut six 3" x 3" A squares from each of the six light–medium green prints.

2. Cut enough 2¼"-wide strips of random lengths from the six light–medium green prints to make 127"-long binding strip.

3. Cut one 17½" x 17½" square from each light–medium green print for napkins.

4. Cut one 2¾" by fabric width strip tan tonal; subcut strip into two 8" B strips and two 13½" F strips.

5. Cut two 2¾" x 34½" C strips tan tonal.

6. Cut two 2¾" x 40½" G strips tan tonal.

7. Cut two 17½" x 17½" squares tan tonal for napkins.

8. Cut one 1" by fabric width strip green mottled; subcut strip into two 1" x 12½" D strips.

9. Cut two 1" x 35½" E strips green mottled.

10. Cut one 2⅜" x 9½" H strip green mottled for each napkin ring.

Runner

Preparing the Appliqué

1. Trace the flower pattern 14 times on the wrong side of the rose print, leaving a margin between each shape.

2. Fold the fabric in half with right sides together with the traced patterns on top; pin to fleece or lightweight batting.

3. Sew all around on traced lines as shown in Figure 1; cut out ⅛" from seam. Trim fleece close to stitching and clip curves.

Figure 1

4. Cut a slash where indicated on the pattern through one layer of fabric only; apply no-fray solution to the cut edges and let dry.

5. Turn right side out through opening; press edges flat.

6. Whipstitch the edges of the opening closed.

7. Hand-quilt or machine topstitch ³⁄₁₆" from edge of each flower.

8. Complete 24 leaves in the same manner using green mottled fabric.

9. Prepare pattern for flower center; cut as directed.

10. Apply no-fray solution to the edges of the flower centers and let dry.

11. Hand-sew gathering stitches around the edge of one flower center; place button face down on wrong side of fabric circle. Pull thread to gather fabric tightly around the button; knot thread and attach button to the center of one stitched flower; knot thread; do not cut off. ***Note:*** *Thread will be* used to attach flower to runner later. Repeat for all flowers/flower centers.

Completing the Top

1. Arrange and join 12 A squares to make a row; repeat to make three rows being careful to arrange so no two like pieces are together; press seams in adjoining rows in opposite directions.

2. Join the rows to complete the pieced center; press seams in one direction.

3. Sew B strips to opposite short ends and C strips to opposite long sides of the pieced center; press seams toward B and C strips.

4. Sew D strips to opposite short ends and E strips to opposite long sides of the pieced center; press seams toward D and E strips.

5. Sew F strips to opposite short ends and G strips to opposite long sides of the pieced center to complete the pieced top; press seams toward F and G strips.

Completing the Runner

1. Sandwich the batting between the completed top and prepared backing; pin or baste layers together.

2. Quilt as desired by hand or machine; remove pins or basting. ***Note:*** *The quilting design used is given with a positioning guide for placement.* Trim excess backing and batting even with runner top.

3. Join binding strips on short ends to make one long strip; press seams open. Fold the strip in half along length with wrong sides together; press.

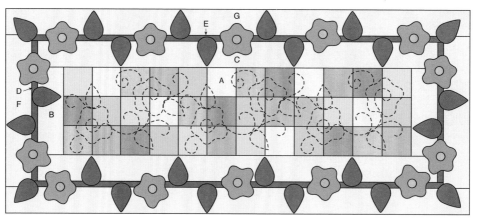

A Garden Square Runner
Placement Diagram 40" x 17½"

Tip

Limit dimensional embellishment in the center of the table runner so you can safely set centerpieces, candlesticks, etc., on the center section.

~Chris Malone

4. Sew binding to the right side of the runner edges, mitering corners and overlapping ends. Fold binding to the back side and stitch in place.

5. Arrange and pin five flowers and eight leaves on each long side and two flowers and two leaves on each short end of the quilted top referring to the Placement Diagram for positioning; pin a leaf at each corner.

6. When satisfied with placement, using the thread left dangling on each flower, hand-stitch flowers in place at the centers.

7. Hand-quilt a line through the length of the center of each leaf to hold in place to finish the runner.

Napkin

1. Pin one each green and tan 17½" x 17½" napkin squares right sides together; sew all around using a ¼" seam allowance, leaving a 3" opening on one side.

2. Trim corners; turn right side out through opening and press edges flat.

3. Fold seam allowance in at opening; hand-stitch opening closed.

4. Topstitch ¼" from edge all around.

5. Repeat for second napkin.

Napkin Ring

1. Prepare two each flowers, leaves and flower centers as for runner. Stitch the flower centers to the flowers.

2. Fold the H strip in half along length with right sides together; stitch ¼" from the long edges. Press seam open and turn right side out; center seam on the back of the tube and press as shown in Figure 2.

Figure 2

3. Insert the piece of elastic into the tube, gathering the tube on the elastic so the ends are even with the tube raw edges as shown in Figure 3; pin to hold.

Figure 3   **Figure 4**

4. Fold the tube in half with seamed side inside and stitch the short ends together as shown in Figure 4; press seam open.

5. Tack the flower to the napkin holder, covering the short seam; tack the leaf to the back side of the flower to finish.

6. Repeat steps 2–5 to complete two napkin rings. ◈

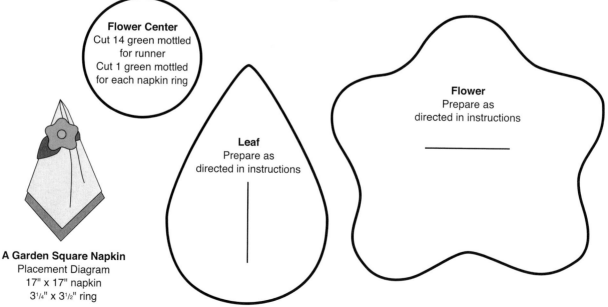

Flower Center
Cut 14 green mottled
for runner
Cut 1 green mottled
for each napkin ring

Leaf
Prepare as
directed in instructions

Flower
Prepare as
directed in instructions

A Garden Square Napkin
Placement Diagram
17" x 17" napkin
3¼" x 3½" ring

Start

Quilting Design & Positioning Pattern
Repeat 3 times down patchwork center;
tendrils are double-stitched. Leaf and
tendril are not repeated on the third set.
Enlarge 125%

Finish

Green Leaves Runner

Design by Chris Malone

Show your green side with the flowing curves
of this runner as your table centerpiece.

Project Specifications
Skill Level: Beginner
Runner Size: 36" x 12"

Materials
- ⅛ yard each 6 olive green prints
- ½ yard dark olive green print
- Batting 42" x 18"
- Backing 42" x 18"
- Dark olive green all-purpose thread
- Quilting thread
- Compass and pencil
- Large piece of paper for pattern (newspaper will do)
- Basic sewing tools and supplies

Cutting
1. From each of the olive green prints, cut the following strips: one 3" x 13", one 2½" x 13" and one 2" x 13".

2. From dark olive green print, cut four 2½"-wide bias strips to total 100" for binding.

3. Prepare template for leaf shape using pattern given. Trace leaf shapes onto the wrong side of the dark olive green print as directed, adding a ¼" seam allowance all around when cutting.

Completing the Top
1. Arrange and join the 13" strips, lining up the long sides and varying widths and prints as shown in Figure 1.

Figure 1

2. To draw the pattern for the runner, fold a piece of paper in half; set the compass to 6" and draw a quarter circle with the point of the compass at the fold on one edge as shown in Figure 2; cut out and unfold to a 12" half-circle.

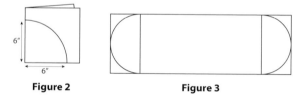

Figure 2   **Figure 3**

3. Tape together plain sheets of paper to make a 12" x 36½" strip; place the half-circle pattern at one end. Trace around the pattern, including the straight edge, and then move the pattern to the other end and repeat as shown in Figure 3.

4. Cut out the rounded edge. Now fold the paper pattern in half crosswise, matching the round ends, and then fold again up to the drawn straight line.

5. Use the pattern given to draw the inner curves on the folded section as shown in Figure 4; cut on the lines and unfold for a full-size pattern for the runner.

Figure 4

6. Pin the paper pattern to the pieced rectangle; cut out. Staystitch ³⁄₁₆" from the cut edge all around to stabilize.

7. Turn under the edges of the leaf shapes using marked lines on the wrong sides as guides; baste to hold.

8. Arrange leaf shapes on the pieced runner top referring to the Placement Diagram and photo of sample project for positioning; hand-stitch in place.

Completing the Runner

1. Sandwich the batting between the completed top and prepared backing; pin or baste layers together to hold.

2. Quilt as desired by hand or machine; remove pins or basting. Trim excess backing and batting even with runner top. ***Note:*** *To duplicate the quilting on the sample, mark the veins on each leaf referring to leaf pattern. Machine-quilt ¼" all around the leaves, quilt the stem and up the vein. Go back down the vein and quilt each V-shaped line.*

3. Join binding strips on short ends to make one long strip; press seams open. Fold the strip in half along length with wrong sides together; press.

4. Sew binding to right side of runner edges, overlapping ends. Fold binding to the back side and stitch in place to finish. ◈

Leaf
Cut 8 dark olive
green print
(reverse 4)

Green Leaves Runner
Placement Diagram 36" x 12"

Fold   Fold

Inner Curve Pattern

Elegant Blue Iris Runner

Design by Barbara Clayton

A Celtic knot design adds elegance to this iris-motif runner.

Four-Blossom Iris
7" x 7" Block
Make 1

One-Blossom Iris
7" x 7" Block
Make 2

Project Specifications
Skill Level: Advanced
Runner Size: 34" x 15"
Block Size: 7" x 7"
Number of Blocks: 3

Materials
- ¼ yard medium blue mottled
- ¼ yard dark blue mottled
- ¼ yard dark green mottled
- ¼ yard light green mottled
- ½ yard navy print
- ⅝ yard tan print
- ⅝ yard cream tonal
- Batting 40" x 21"
- Backing 40" x 21"
- All-purpose thread to match fabrics
- Clear .004 invisible thread
- Cream, light and dark blue, and light and dark green rayon thread
- Tan quilting thread
- 1½ yards 12"-wide fusible web
- 1 yard fabric stabilizer
- Water-erasable marker
- Basic sewing tools and supplies

Cutting
1. Cut one 7½" by fabric width strip cream tonal; subcut strip into three 7½" x 7½" A squares.

2. Cut two 2¾" x 30⅛" D strips cream tonal.

3. Cut one 2¾" by fabric width strip cream tonal; subcut strip into two 14⅞" E strips.

4. Cut three 2¼" by fabric width strips tan print for binding.

5. Cut one 11¼" by fabric width strip navy print; subcut strip into one 11¼" square. Cut this square in half on both diagonal to make four B triangles.

6. Trim remainder of the 11¼" strip to 5⅞"; subcut into two 5⅞" squares. Cut each square in half on one diagonal to make four C triangles.

7. Trace appliqué shapes given onto the paper side of the fusible web as directed on patterns for number to cut; cut out shapes, leaving a margin around each one. ***Note:*** *Cut Celtic design open areas away, leaving each motif as one piece. Dotted lines indicate stitching lines that will give the woven appearance to the design when finished.*

8. Fuse shapes to the wrong side of mottled fabrics as directed on pattern; cut out shapes on traced lines. Remove paper backing.

Completing the Appliqué

1. Fold and crease the A square twice diagonally to find center; center and fuse the four-blossom iris design with pieces in numerical order on one A square referring to the block drawing for positioning.

2. Repeat step 1, centering a one-blossom iris design on each of the remaining two A squares.

3. Arrange and fuse side Celtic design on each B triangle and the corner Celtic design on the C triangles with the straight edges of the designs ⅞" from the edges of the triangles as shown in Figure 1.

⅞"   ⅞"   ⅞"

B   C

Figure 1

4. Cut seven 7" x 7" squares fabric stabilizer; cut four of the squares in half on one diagonal. Pin a stabilizer square or triangle to the wrong side of each fused area.

5. Using a close satin zigzag stitch and matching rayon thread in the top of the machine and matching all-purpose thread in the bobbin, stitch around each fused shape.

6. Remove fabric stabilizer.

Completing the Top

1. Arrange and join the appliquéd blocks with the B and C triangles in diagonal rows as shown in Figure 2; press seams toward blocks.

Figure 2

2. Sew D strips to opposite long sides and E strips to opposite short ends of the pieced center; press seams toward D and E strips.

3. Center, arrange and fuse six border iris motifs in numerical order to each long side and two motifs in numerical order to each short end of the pieced center referring to the Placement Diagram for positioning of motifs.

Side Celtic Motif
Cut 4 tan print

4. Cut (16) 2½" x 5½" rectangles fabric stabilizer; pin one in place behind each border motif. Stitch motifs in place as in step 5 for Completing the Appliqué to complete the pieced top.

Completing the Runner

1. Sandwich the batting between the completed top and prepared backing; pin or baste layers together to hold.

2. Quilt as desired by hand or machine; remove pins or basting. Trim excess backing and batting even with runner top. **Note:** *The sample was hand-quilted ¼" from edges of appliqué motifs and seam in blocks, on borders and close to motifs in the B and C triangles using tan quilting thread. It was machine-quilted in the ditch of seams with invisible thread.*

3. Join binding strips on short ends to make one long strip; press seams open. Fold the strip in half along length with wrong sides together; press.

4. Sew binding to right side of runner edges, mitering corners and overlapping ends. Fold binding to the back side and stitch in place to finish. ◈

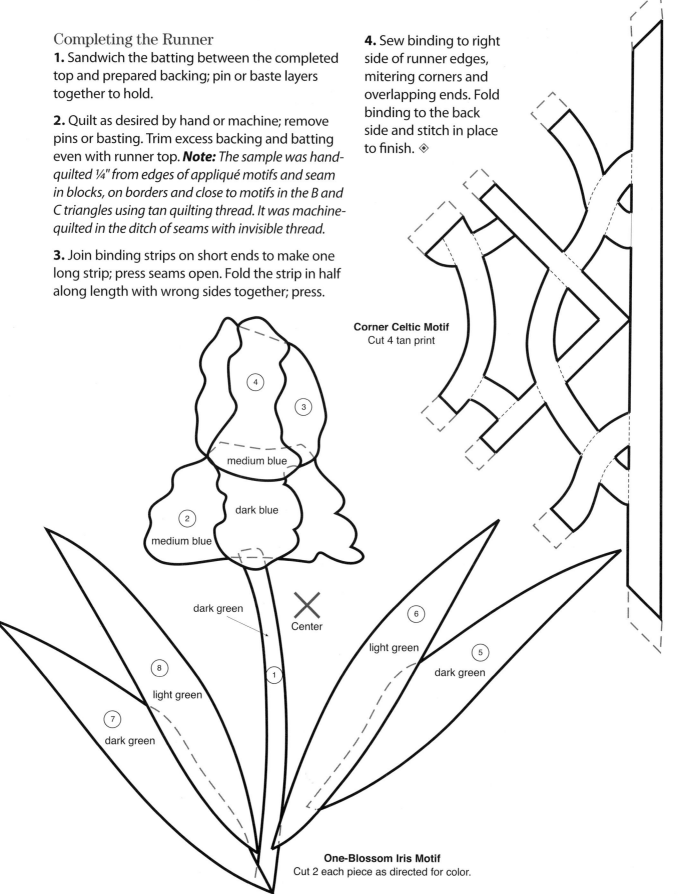

Corner Celtic Motif
Cut 4 tan print

medium blue

dark blue

medium blue

dark green

Center

light green

dark green

light green

dark green

One-Blossom Iris Motif
Cut 2 each piece as directed for color.

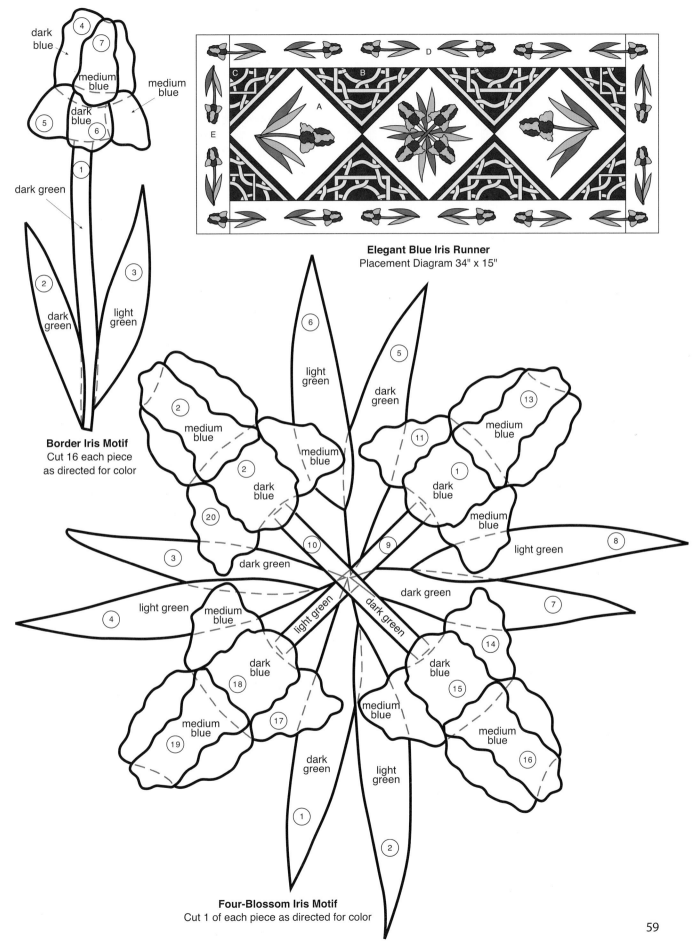

dark blue

medium blue

medium blue

dark blue

dark green

dark green

light green

Border Iris Motif
Cut 16 each piece
as directed for color

Elegant Blue Iris Runner
Placement Diagram 34" x 15"

light green

dark green

medium blue

medium blue

dark blue

medium blue

dark blue

medium blue

light green

light green

dark green

light green

dark green

medium blue

dark blue

dark blue

medium blue

medium blue

dark blue

medium blue

dark green

light green

Four-Blossom Iris Motif
Cut 1 of each piece as directed for color

Roses & Rosebuds Runner

Design by Jodi Warner

Tiny paper-pieced rosebuds combine with appliquéd roses in this open-center runner.

Project Specifications
Skill Level: Advanced
Runner Size: 47" x 17"

Materials
- Scraps 4 different shades of rose/burgundy solids or tonals
- Fat eighth dark green tonal
- Fat eighth medium green tonal
- ⅛ yard dark peach print
- ⅛ yard medium rose tonal
- ¼ yard peach print 1
- ⅜ yard peach/tan stripe
- ½ yard peach print 2
- Thin batting 50" x 20"
- Backing 50" x 20"
- All-purpose thread to match fabrics
- Quilting thread
- ⅜ yard fusible web
- ⅓ yard fabric stabilizer
- Appliqué pressing sheet
- ¼" bias bar
- Basic sewing tools and supplies

Cutting
1. Cut one 4¼" by fabric width strip peach/tan stripe. Prepare template for G using pattern given; cut two G pieces from the strip. Transfer outer corner dots.

2. Cut three 1¾" by fabric width strips peach/tan stripe; subcut strips into four 12" K, two 13" L and two 15" M strips.

3. Cut one 6½" x 30½" A piece peach print 1.

4. Cut one 9⅜" x 9⅜" square peach print 2; cut in half on one diagonal to make two F triangles.

5. Cut two 1½" by fabric width strips peach print 2; subcut strip into four 2½" B, (16) 3¼" C and four 1¼" D pieces.

6. Cut one 2½" by fabric width strip peach print 2; subcut strip into two 10½" E pieces.

7. Cut three ⅞" by fabric width strips dark peach print; subcut strips into two 35" H strips, two 10" I strips and two 11" J strips.

8. Cut four 12"-long 1⅛"-wide bias strips medium green tonal for vines.

9. Make copies of each paper-piecing pattern as directed with patterns. Cut up one copy of each pattern to make templates for each numbered piece. Cut fabric pieces using templates, adding a ¼" seam all around each piece and placing the patterns printed side up on the wrong side of the fabrics when cutting; label and keep pieces for each pattern together in envelopes to keep them from being mixed up later.

10. Trace individual appliqué shapes onto the paper side of the fusible web as directed on pieces for number to cut; cut out shapes, leaving a margin around each one.

11. Fuse shapes to the wrong side of fabric scraps as directed on patterns for color; cut out shapes on traced lines. Remove paper backing. ***Note:*** *Keep pieces for each rose motif together to avoid confusion later when fusing to F and G pieces.*

Completing the Rosebud Units

1. Set stitch length to 18–20 stitches per inch; change needle to size 90—the larger needle will help perforate the paper and make paper removal easier.

2. Select one paper-piecing pattern and previously cut fabric patches. Lay piece 1 right side up over space 1 on the unprinted side of the paper pattern, with one longer raw edge of piece 1 extending beyond the seam line between pieces 1 and 2 as shown in Figure 1.

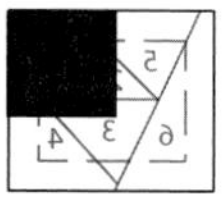

Figure 1

3. Pin piece 2 right sides together with piece 1 along the ½ line.

4. Flip pinned paper pattern over and sew on the line between spaces 1 and 2, extending stitches slightly into space 3 and to the outside edge of the pattern as shown in Figure 2. Clip threads and press piece 2 to the right side; check to be sure spaces 1 and 2 are completely covered before adding piece 3.

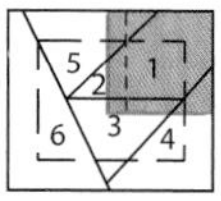

Figure 2

5. Continue adding pieces in numerical order until the paper pattern is complete; press without steam. Use a rotary cutter to trim outer edges exactly on the outermost cutting lines of pattern with the paper side up.

6. Repeat steps 2–5 to complete 10 each right and left paper-pieced buds; remove paper and set aside.

Completing the Paper-Pieced Panels

1. Join two right paper-pieced buds with one B and two C pieces to make a B-C strip as shown in Figure 3; press seams toward B and C pieces.

Figure 3

2. Join three left paper-pieced buds with one D and two C pieces to make a C-D strip as shown in Figure 4; press seams toward C and D pieces.

Figure 4

3. Sew the B-C strip to the C-D strip to complete a left-side panel as shown in Figure 5; press seams in one direction. Repeat to make two left-side panels.

Left-Side Panel
Make 2

Figure 5

4. Join two left paper-pieced buds with one B and two C pieces to make a B-C strip referring to Figure 6; press seams toward B and C pieces.

Right-Side Panel
Make 2

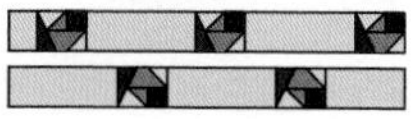

Figure 6

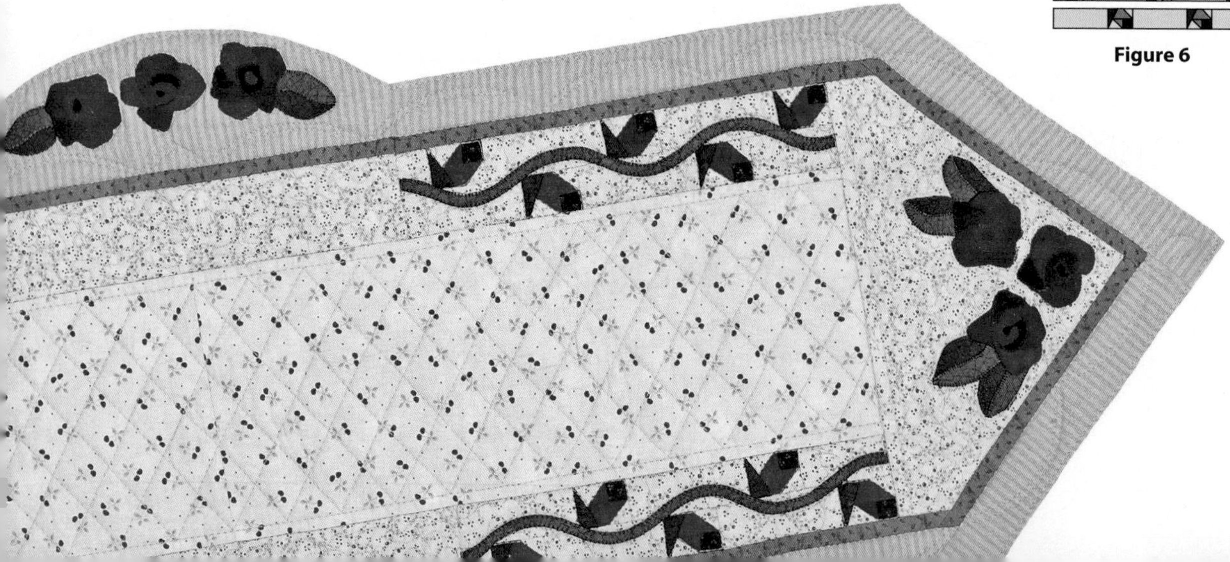

5. Join three right paper-pieced buds with one D and two C pieces to make a C-D strip, again referring to Figure 6; press seams toward C and D pieces.

6. Sew the B-C strip to the C-D strip to complete a right-side panel, again referring to Figure 6; press seams in one direction. Repeat to make two right-side panels.

7. Fold each bias strip with wrong sides together along length; stitch a scant ¼" seam along the long raw edge. Trim seam to ⅛".

8. Insert the ¼" bias bar inside each strip and press with seam open and centered on the back side to complete bias vines as shown in Figure 7.

Figure 7

9. Arrange and machine edge-stitch one bias vine on each side panel in a curving design using curved vine pattern given and matching dots on pattern to corners of bud units as shown in Figure 8.

Figure 8

Completing the Appliqué

1. Using the appliqué pressing sheet, layer pieces for one rose motif in numerical order and fuse to complete one motif; repeat to complete all rose motifs.

2. Arrange and fuse one center and one each side and reverse side rose motifs on G pieces referring to positioning lines given on pattern.

3. Arrange and fuse one center and one each end and reverse end rose motifs on F ½" from edges at the square corner of each triangle as shown in Figure 9.

Figure 9

4. Cut fabric stabilizer to fit behind each fused area.

5. Using thread to match one of the fabrics and a machine-overcast stitch, stitch over all exposed edges. When stitching is complete on all pieces, remove fabric stabilizer.

Completing the Top

1. Join one left and one right side panel with E to make a side strip as shown in Figure 10; press seams toward E. Repeat to make two side strips.

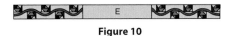

Figure 10

2. Sew a side strip to opposite long sides of A referring to Figure 11 for placement of panels.

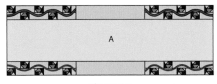

Figure 11

3. Center and sew an appliquéd F triangle to each end of the stitched center; press seams toward F. Trim excess F at each edge as shown in Figure 12.

Figure 12

4. Center and sew an H strip to opposite long sides of the pieced center; press seams toward H strips.

5. Using a straightedge, trim excess H at each end even with the edge of F as shown in Figure 13.

Figure 13

6. Add I and then J to angled ends; press seams toward I and J strips. Trim angles as in step 5.

7. Join two K pieces with G to make a G-K strip as shown in Figure 14; press seams toward G. Repeat to make two G-K strips.

Figure 14

8. Center and sew a G-K strip to opposite long sides of the pieced center; press seams toward H strips. Trim angles at ends as in step 5.

9. Add L and then M to angled ends; press seams toward L and M strips. Trim angles as in step 5 to complete the runner top.

Completing the Runner

1. Sandwich batting between the completed top and prepared backing piece; baste or pin layers together.

2. Quilt as desired by hand or machine; do not quilt in outside border. **Note:** *The runner shown was machine-quilted in a diamond pattern in the center A piece, along the edge of the bias in the paper-pieced units and in a meandering pattern in appliquéd end units.*

3. Trim excess backing only even with top edges; trim batting ¼" narrower than top all around.

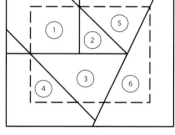

Figure 15

4. Turn ¼" under on top and back edges; hand-stitch edges together invisibly as shown in Figure 15. Quilt ⅛" from outer edge all around and add decorative quilting in outer borders to finish. ◈

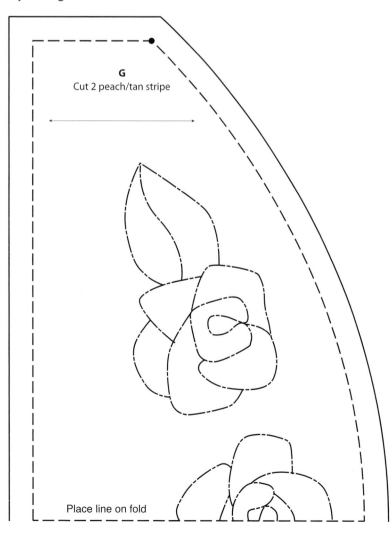

G
Cut 2 peach/tan stripe

Place line on fold

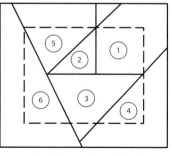

Right Paper-Pieced Bud
Make 11 copies

Left Paper-Pieced Bud
Make 11 copies

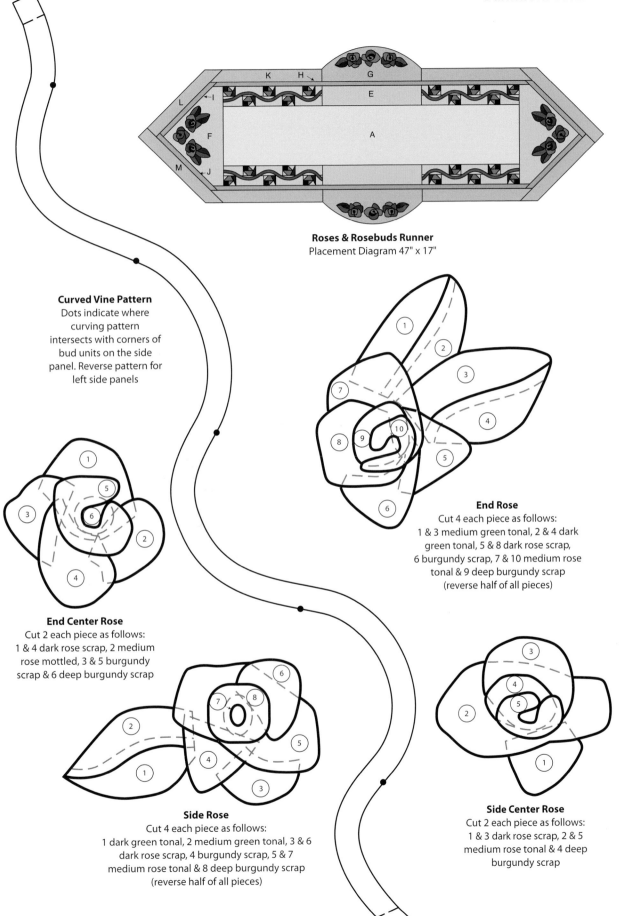

Roses & Rosebuds Runner
Placement Diagram 47" x 17"

Curved Vine Pattern
Dots indicate where curving pattern intersects with corners of bud units on the side panel. Reverse pattern for left side panels

End Rose
Cut 4 each piece as follows:
1 & 3 medium green tonal, 2 & 4 dark green tonal, 5 & 8 dark rose scrap, 6 burgundy scrap, 7 & 10 medium rose tonal & 9 deep burgundy scrap (reverse half of all pieces)

End Center Rose
Cut 2 each piece as follows:
1 & 4 dark rose scrap, 2 medium rose mottled, 3 & 5 burgundy scrap & 6 deep burgundy scrap

Side Rose
Cut 4 each piece as follows:
1 dark green tonal, 2 medium green tonal, 3 & 6 dark rose scrap, 4 burgundy scrap, 5 & 7 medium rose tonal & 8 deep burgundy scrap (reverse half of all pieces)

Side Center Rose
Cut 2 each piece as follows:
1 & 3 dark rose scrap, 2 & 5 medium rose tonal & 4 deep burgundy scrap

Reindeer in the Pines

Design by Barbara Clayton

Recall winter days in the woods with this two-color runner.

Project Specification
Skill Level: Intermediate
Runner Size: 32" x 15"

Materials
- ½ yard white solid
- 1 yard green solid
- Batting 38" x 21"
- Backing 38" x 21"
- All-purpose thread to match fabrics
- Clear .004 thread
- Green rayon thread
- Green quilting thread
- ½ yard 12"-wide fusible web
- ⅓ yard fabric stabilizer
- Water-erasable marker
- Basic sewing tools and supplies and water-erasable marker

Cutting
1. Cut one 8½" x 25½" A rectangle white solid.

2. Cut two 1⅞" by fabric width strips each white (B) and green (C) solids; subcut strips into 35 each 1⅞" squares each fabric.

3. Cut three 3" by fabric width strips white solid; subcut strips into two 27½" D strips and two 15½" E strips.

4. Cut 2¼"-wide bias strips green solid to total 110".

5. Trace appliqué shapes given onto the paper side of the fusible web as directed on patterns for number to cut; cut out shapes, leaving a margin around each one.

6. Fuse shapes to the wrong side of fabrics as directed on pattern; cut out shapes on traced lines. Remove paper backing.

Completing the Appliqué
1. Arrange and fuse the tree shapes on A with bottom bough of green ⅝" from the side edge and trunk 1⅛" from the bottom edge referring to Figure 1 for positioning.

Figure 1

2. Arrange and fuse the deer shapes on A with antlers ½" from the side edge and hooves ¾" from the bottom edge, again referring to Figure 1 for positioning.

3. Cut two 8" x 8" squares fabric stabilizer; pin a square behind each fused area.

4. Using a close satin zigzag stitch and green rayon thread in the top of the machine and matching all-purpose thread in the bobbin, stitch around each tree and deer shape.

5. Remove fabric stabilizer.

Completing the Top
1. Draw a diagonal line from corner to corner on the wrong side of each B square.

2. Place a B square right sides together with a C square and stitch ¼" on each side of the marked line as shown in Figure 2. Repeat with all B and C squares.

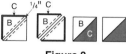

Figure 2

3. Cut apart on the marked lines and press units open with seam toward C to complete 70 B-C units, again referring to Figure 2.

4. Join eight B-C units to make an end strip referring to Figure 3 for positioning of units; press seams in one direction. Repeat to make two end strips.

Figure 3

5. Sew an end strip to opposite short ends of the appliquéd A center referring to the Placement Diagram for positioning; press seams toward A.

6. Join 27 B-C units to make a side strip referring to Figure 4 for positioning of units, being careful to place the first two units in the right position; press seams in one direction. Repeat to make two side strips.

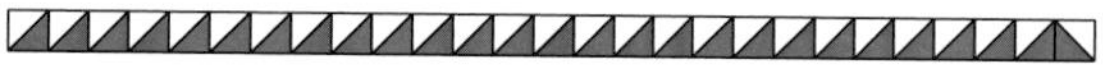

Figure 4

7. Sew the side strips to opposite long sides of the appliquéd A center referring to the Placement Diagram for positioning; press seams toward A.

8. Sew D strips to opposite long sides and E strips to opposite short ends of the pieced center to complete the runner top; press seams toward D and E strips.

Completing the Runner

1. Mark quilting design given onto the D and E borders and a ¾" diagonal grid through the center A piece using the water-erasable marker.

2. Sandwich the batting between the completed top and prepared backing; pin or baste layers together to hold.

3. Quilt on marked lines and as desired by hand or machine; remove pins or basting. **Note:** *The sample is quilted in the ditch between border seams using clear thread.* Trim excess backing and batting even with runner top.

4. Trace the scallop pattern on white paper; cut out along line.

5. Lay the pattern on a corner of the runner with outside curves of the scallops meeting the edge of the runner top; trace the pattern onto the top. Repeat for the other three corners, flipping the pattern for the two opposite sides. Use the scallops on the pattern to fill in the center 9" of each side. Trim the runner edges on the marked lines.

6. Join binding strips on short ends to make one long strip; press seams open. Fold the strip in half along length with wrong sides together; press.

7. Sew binding to right side of runner edges overlapping ends. Fold binding to the back side and hand-stitch in place to finish. ◈

Scallop Pattern

Reindeer in the Pines
Placement Diagram 32" x 15"

Quilting Design

Tree
Cut 2 green solid

Reindeer
Cut 2 green solid

Driving Me Crazy Runner & Napkin Ring

Design by Chris Malone

Make this colorful runner with matching napkin and napkin ring to create a festive mood.

- -

Project Specifications
Skill Level: Beginner
Runner Size: 44½" x 14½"
Napkin Size: 15½" x 15½"
Napkin Ring Size: 3½" x 4½"

Materials
- 2 fat quarters red tonals for each napkin
- 6–8 fat quarters or scraps assorted red tonals or mottleds for runner
- 17" x 48" pre-shrunk and pressed muslin
- ⅛ yard green print
- ¼ yard black-with-white print
- ½ yard white-with-black print
- Batting 51" x 21" and scrap for napkin rings
- Backing 51" x 21"
- Red and all-purpose thread to match appliqué fabrics
- 1 yard 18"-wide lightweight fusible web
- 1¼ yards fabric stabilizer
- Medium-large snap for each napkin ring
- ⅞"-diameter yellow button for each napkin ring
- Basic sewing tools and supplies

Cutting
Note: *There are no set sizes for the crazy-patch piece; it is made with random odd-shaped fabric swatches. Use a slightly longer than normal stitch length and do not backstitch on the seams.*

1. Trace the large leaf and large flower circles onto the paper side of the fusible web as directed on patterns for number to cut; cut out shapes, leaving a margin around each one. Repeat with one small flower center for each napkin ring.

2. Fuse shapes to the wrong sides of fabrics as directed on pieces for color; cut out shapes on traced lines. Remove paper backing.

3. Cut four 2¼" by fabric width strips white-with-black print for runner binding.

4. For each napkin, cut one each 13" x 13" (A) and 16" x 16" (B) squares red tonals.

5. For each napkin, cut four 2" x 13" C strips white-with-black print.

6. For each napkin, cut four 2" x 2" D squares black-with-white print.

7. For each napkin ring, cut one 2½" x 8½" E strip black-with-white print.

Runner
Completing the Top

1. Cut a three- or five-sided piece of red fabric; place it right side up roughly in the center of the muslin background as shown in Figure 1.

Figure 1

2. Cut and place a second piece of red fabric right sides together with the first piece; sew a ¼" seam on one edge as shown in Figure 2. Press the top piece to the right side. Trim edges even with the first piece.

Figure 2

3. Continue adding pieces clockwise around the first fabric, using a variety of prints and shapes as shown in Figure 3.

Figure 3

4. Continue adding fabric until the muslin is covered, trimming seams to ¼" after each addition as necessary. ***Note:*** *You may need to clip a few stitches to release the fabric for trimming if another seam has crossed over it. Sometimes you may wish to seam two swatches together before adding them to the foundation if needed. You may also need to fold under a ¼" seam allowance and hand-stitch it with an invisible appliqué stitch to prevent an exposed raw edge.*

5. When the background is completely covered, trim to 45" x 15"; machine-stitch ³⁄₁₆" from the edges to secure seams.

6. Complete the circle appliqué motifs, layering as in pattern.

7. Arrange and fuse the circle motifs with large leaves on the completed background referring to the Placement Diagram for positioning.

8. Cut fabric stabilizer pieces to fit behind each fused shape.

9. Using thread to match fabrics and a machine buttonhole stitch, stitch around edges of each fused shape to complete the runner top.

Completing the Runner

1. Sandwich the batting between the completed top and prepared backing; pin or baste layers together.

2. Quilt as desired by hand or machine; remove pins or basting. Trim excess backing and batting even with runner top.

3. Join binding strips on short ends to make one long strip; press seams open. Fold the strip in half along length with wrong sides together; press.

4. Sew binding to the right side of the runner edges, mitering corners and overlapping ends. Fold binding to the back side and stitch in place to finish.

Napkin

1. To complete one napkin, sew a C strip to opposite sides of A; press seams toward C.

2. Sew D to each end of the remaining two C strips; press seams toward C. Add these strips to the remaining sides of the A-C unit to complete the napkin front.

Driving Me Crazy
Placement Diagram 44½" x 14½"

3. Place the pieced napkin front right sides together with the B square; stitch all around, leaving a 3" opening on one side. Turn right side out through opening; press edges flat. Hand-stitch opening closed to finish.

Napkin Rings

1. For each napkin ring, trace small flower circle pattern onto the wrong side of the black-with-white print; fold fabric in half with right sides together with pattern on top.

2. Pin scrap of batting to the layered fabrics; sew all around. Referring to Figure 4, cut out ⅛" from seam and trim fleece close to seam; clip curves and make a slash through one layer only of the fabric. Turn flower right side out through slash and press. Whipstitch the cut edges of the slash together.

1/8"

Figure 4

3. Repeat steps 1 and 2 to complete one leaf for each napkin ring except leave bottom straight edge open for turning, then turn edges in and whipstitch closed.

4. Fuse a small flower center to each flower circle; straight-stitch close to edge of center circle. Straight-stitch along the center of each leaf.

5. Fold the E strip in half with right sides together along the length; sew along long and short edges, leaving a 2" opening on the long side. Trim corners and turn right side out; press. Fold in seam allowance at opening and hand-stitch closed.

6. Overlap the short edges 1", and sew a snap closure to the ends.

7. Sew the yellow button to the flower center and with same thread, attach the flower to one end of napkin ring. Tuck leaf under edge of flower and tack in place to finish. ◈

Napkin Ring
Placement Diagram 3½" x 4½"

Napkin
Placement Diagram 15½" x 15½"

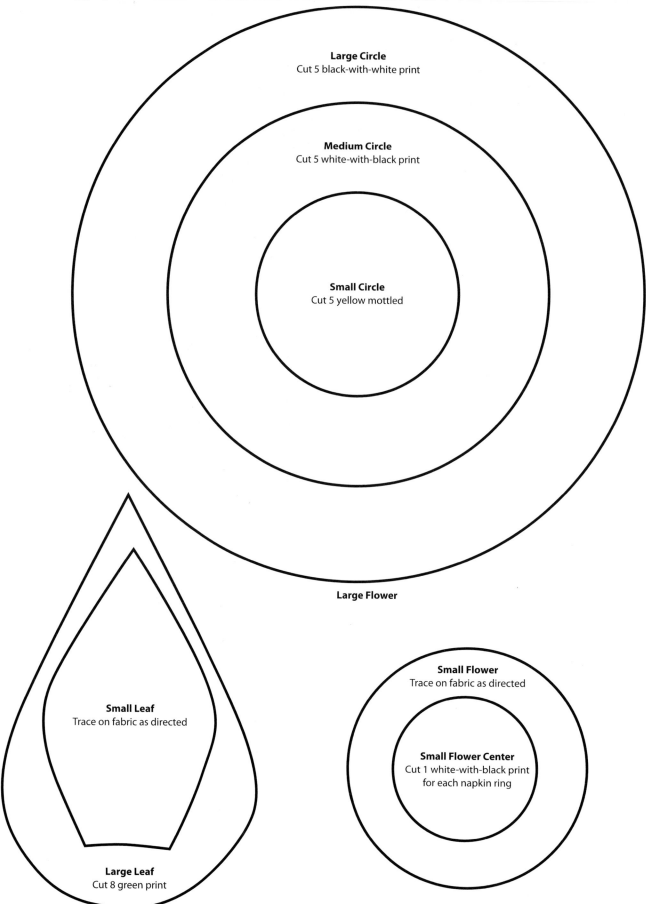

Large Circle
Cut 5 black-with-white print

Medium Circle
Cut 5 white-with-black print

Small Circle
Cut 5 yellow mottled

Large Flower

Small Leaf
Trace on fabric as directed

Large Leaf
Cut 8 green print

Small Flower
Trace on fabric as directed

Small Flower Center
Cut 1 white-with-black print
for each napkin ring

Contemporary Looks

If you like designs that are a little uncommon, look at the
runners in this chapter. These runners are patchwork,
but they have the look of today for those quilters
who want a runner that is a little unique.

Four-Panel Table Runner

Design by Phyllis Dobbs

Cover every side of the table with this four-part table runner.

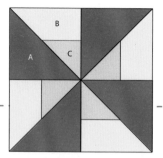

Pinwheel
10" x 10" Block
Make 5

Project Specifications

Skill Level: Beginner
Runner Size: 62" x 62"
Block Size: 10" x 10"
Number of Blocks: 5

Materials

- ¼ yard gold print
- ⅓ yard coordinating stripe
- ½ yard gold tonal
- ½ yard gold floral
- 1 yard green print
- 1 (16" x 68") and 2 (16" x 29") rectangles batting
- 1 (16" x 68") and 2 (16" x 29") rectangles backing
- Neutral-color all-purpose thread
- Quilting thread
- Basic sewing tools and supplies

Cutting

1. Cut one 10½" by fabric width strip gold floral; subcut strip into four 10½" D squares.

2. Cut two 5⅞" by fabric width strips gold tonal; subcut strips into (20) 2¾" B rectangles. Cut each B rectangle from the right end diagonally from the bottom corner to the top edge at a 45-degree angle as shown in Figure 1.

Figure 1

3. Cut one 3⅝" by fabric width strip gold print; subcut strip into (10) 3⅝" squares. Cut each square in half on one diagonal to make 20 C triangles.

4. Cut two 5⅞" by fabric width strips green print; subcut strips into (10) 5⅞" squares. Cut each square in half on one diagonal to make 20 A triangles.

5. Cut seven 2¼" by fabric width strips green print for binding.

6. Cut three 2½" by fabric width strips coordinating stripe; subcut strip into (12) 10½" E strips.

Completing the Blocks

1. Sew B to C to make a B-C unit as shown in Figure 2; press seam toward C. Repeat to make 20 B-C units.

Figure 2

2. Sew a B-C unit to A to complete an A-B-C unit as shown in Figure 3; press seam toward A. Repeat to make 20 A-B-C units.

Figure 3

3. To complete one Pinwheel block, join two A-B-C units to make a row as shown in Figure 4; repeat to make two rows. Press seams in opposite directions.

Figure 4

4. Join the rows referring to the block drawing to complete one block; press seam in one direction.

5. Repeat steps 3 and 4 to complete five Pinwheel blocks.

Completing the Top

1. Join one Pinwheel block with one D square and three E strips to make a side unit as shown in Figure 5; press seams toward E. Repeat to make four side units.

Figure 5

2. Sew a side unit to each side of the remaining Pinwheel block to complete the runner top.

Completing the Runner

1. Center and sew a 16" x 29" backing piece to opposite sides of the 16" x 68" backing piece to make a backing piece to match the pieced top as shown in Figure 6; repeat with batting pieces.

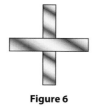

Figure 6

2. Sandwich the batting between the completed top and prepared backing; pin or baste layers together.

3. Quilt as desired by hand or machine; remove pins or basting. Trim excess backing and batting even with runner top.

4. Join binding strips on short ends to make one long strip; press seams open. Fold the strip in half along length with wrong sides together; press.

5. Sew binding to the right side of the runner edges, mitering corners and overlapping ends. Fold binding to the back side and stitch in place to finish. ◈

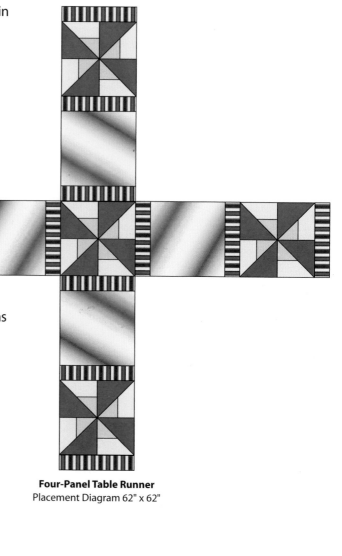

Four-Panel Table Runner
Placement Diagram 62" x 62"

Any Which Way

Design by Julie Weaver

Select a variety of scraps from the same color family and have fun making this runner.

Any Which Way
5½" x 5½" Block
Make 12

Project Specifications
Skill Level: Beginner
Runner Size: 54" x 18"
Block Size: 5½" x 5½"
Number of Blocks: 12

Materials
- Variety of brown scraps
- ¼ yard dark brown print
- ⅔ yard foundation fabric
- ¾ yard brown tonal
- Batting 60" x 24"
- Backing 60" x 24"
- Neutral-color all-purpose thread
- Quilting thread
- Basic sewing tools and supplies

Cutting
1. Cut all brown scraps into 1½"-wide strips.

2. Cut three 7" by fabric width strips foundation fabric; subcut strips into (14) 7" squares.

3. Cut four 1½" by fabric width A/B/C strips dark brown print. Trim to make two each 36" A, 12" B and 14" C strips.

4. Cut four 3" by fabric width D/E/F strips brown mottled. Trim to make two each 39" D, 17" E and 20" F strips.

5. Cut four 2¼" by fabric width strips brown mottled for binding.

Completing the Blocks
1. To make one Any Which Way block, lay a 1½"-wide brown scrap strip diagonally, right side up on one of the 7" foundation squares as shown in Figure 1; trim to a workable length, if necessary.

Figure 1

2. Place a second strip right sides together on the first strip, adjusting the second strip slightly so it doesn't match the edge of the first strip as shown in Figure 2; stitch along the raw edge of the second strip when satisfied with placement. Trim seam allowance to ¼".

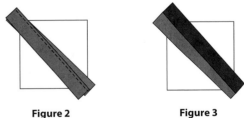

Figure 2   **Figure 3**

3. Flip the second strip to the right side and press flat as shown in Figure 3.

4. Place another strip right sides together with the stitched second strip, adjusting the third strip slightly so it doesn't match the edge of the second strip; trim. Sew the third strip in place; trim, if necessary. Flip right side up and press strip flat.

5. Continue the process until the entire foundation square is covered.

6. Repeat steps to complete 14 stitched squares.

7. Trim 12 of the stitched squares to 6" x 6" as shown in Figure 4 to complete the Any Which Way blocks.

Figure 5

Figure 4

8. Trim the remaining two stitched squares to 6⅜" x 6⅜" square; cut each block in half diagonally across the pieced strips as shown in Figure 5 to make four end triangles.

Completing the Top

1. Join six Any Which Way blocks as shown in Figure 6 to make a row; repeat to make two rows. Press seams in one direction.

Figure 6

2. Join the rows referring to the Placement Diagram; press seam in one direction.

3. Join two end triangles to make an end unit as shown in Figure 7; press seam to one side. Repeat to make two end units.

Figure 7

4. Center and sew an end unit to each short end of the joined rows to complete the pieced center; press seams toward the end units.

5. Center and sew an A strip to opposite long sides of the pieced center; press seams toward A.

6. Using a straightedge, trim excess A at each end to match the angle of the end units as shown in Figure 8.

Figure 8

7. Repeat steps 5 and 6 with B–F strips, referring to the Placement Diagram for positioning of strips, trimming after adding each strip to match angles of ends to complete the pieced top; press seams toward the most recently added strip after each addition.

Completing the Runner

1. Sandwich the batting between the completed top and prepared backing; pin or baste layers together.

2. Quilt as desired by hand or machine; remove pins or basting. Trim excess backing and batting even with runner top.

3. Join binding strips on short ends to make one long strip; press seams open. Fold the strip in half along length with wrong sides together; press.

4. Sew binding to the right side of the runner edges, mitering corners and overlapping ends. Fold binding to the back side and stitch in place to finish. ◈

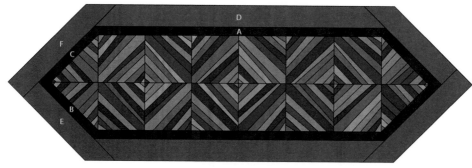

Any Which Way
Placement Diagram 54" x 18"

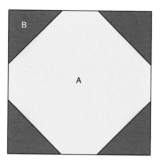

Snowball
4" x 4" Block
Make 16

Sunshine Buttons

Design by Chris Malone

Warm your room with this cheery runner.

Project Specifications
Skill Level: Beginner
Runner Size: 32" x 12"
Block Size: 4" x 4"
Number of Blocks: 16

Materials
- ⅜ yard yellow print
- ½ yard blue print
- Batting 38" x 18"
- Backing 38" x 18"
- Neutral-color all-purpose thread
- Quilting thread
- 16 (¹³⁄₁₆") blue buttons
- Basic sewing tools and supplies

Cutting
1. Cut two 4½" by fabric width strips yellow print; subcut strips into (16) 4½" A squares.

2. Cut three 1¾" by fabric width strips blue print; subcut strips into (64) 1¾" B squares.

3. Cut three 2¼" by fabric width strips blue print for binding.

Completing the Blocks
1. Draw a diagonal line from corner to corner on the wrong side of each B square.

2. Place a B square right sides together on each corner of A and stitch on the marked lines as shown in Figure 1; trim seam to ¼" and press B to the right side to complete one Snowball block, again referring to Figure 1. Repeat

to make 16 Snowball blocks, pressing seams toward A in eight blocks and toward B in the remaining eight blocks.

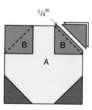

Figure 1

Completing the Top
1. Join four blocks to make the top row, alternating the seam-pressing direction; repeat to make the bottom row.

2. Join the remaining eight blocks to make the center row, alternating the seam pressing direction from that used in the top and bottom rows.

3. Sew the top and bottom rows to the center row to complete the pieced top.

Completing the Runner
1. Sandwich the batting between the completed top and prepared backing; pin or baste layers together.

Sunshine Buttons
Placement Diagram 32" x 12"

2. Quilt as desired by hand or machine; remove pins or basting. Trim excess backing and batting even with runner top.

3. Join binding strips on short ends to make one long strip; press seams open. Fold the strip in half along length with wrong sides together; press.

4. Sew binding to the right side of the runner edges, mitering corners and overlapping ends. Fold binding to the back side and stitch in place.

5. Sew a button in the center of each block to complete the runner. ◈

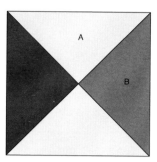

Hourglass
7" x 7" Block
Make 6

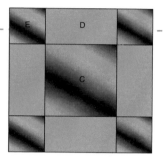

Uneven Nine-Patch
7" x 7" Block
Make 6

Project Specifications

Skill Level: Beginner
Runner Size: 53" x 25"
Block Size: 7" x 7"
Number of Blocks: 12

Materials

- 3–8¼" x 8¼" scrap batik squares for B
- 1 fat quarter black tree-print batik
- 1 fat quarter dark gold batik
- ⅓ yard brown batik
- ⅜ yard cream batik
- 1⅛ yards terra-cotta batik
- Batting 59" x 31"
- Backing 59" x 31"
- Neutral-color all-purpose thread
- Quilting thread
- Basic sewing tools and supplies

Cutting

1. Cut each B square in half on both diagonals as shown in Figure 1 to make 12 B triangles.

Figure 1

Colors of Autumn

Design by Julia Dunn

Rich hues of the season bring to mind
crackling fires, apple cider and falling leaves.

2. Cut one 8¼" by fabric width strip cream batik; subcut strip into three 8¼" squares. Cut each square in half on both diagonals to make 12 A squares.

3. Fussy-cut six 4" x 4" C squares black tree-print batik, centering motifs in squares.

4. Cut three 2¼" x 21" strips black tree-print batik; subcut strips into (24) 2¼" E squares.

5. Cut three 4" x 21" strips dark gold batik; subcut strips into (24) 2¼" D pieces.

6. Cut two 2½" x 42½" F strips brown batik.

7. Cut two 2½" x 18½" G strips brown batik.

8. Cut three 4" by fabric width strips terra-cotta batik. Join strips on short ends to make one long strip; press seams open. Subcut strip into two 46½" H strips.

9. Cut two 4" x 25½" I strips terra-cotta batik.

10. Cut five 2¼" binding strips terra-cotta batik.

Completing the Hourglass Blocks

1. Sew an A triangle to a B triangle as shown in Figure 2; press seam toward B. Repeat to make 12 A-B units.

Figure 2

2. To complete one Hourglass block, join two A-B units referring to the block drawing; press seam in one direction.

3. Repeat step 2 to complete six Hourglass blocks.

Completing the Uneven Nine-Patch Blocks

1. To complete one Uneven Nine-Patch block, sew D to opposite sides of C to make a C-D unit as shown in Figure 3; press seams toward D.

Figure 3

2. Sew E to opposite ends of each D rectangle to make a D-E unit as shown in Figure 4; press seams toward D. Repeat to make two D-E units.

Figure 4

3. Sew a D-E unit to opposite sides of the C-D unit to complete one block referring to the block drawing; press seams away from the C-D unit.

4. Repeat steps 1–3 to complete six Uneven Nine-Patch blocks.

Completing the Top

1. Arrange and join three each Hourglass and Uneven Nine-Patch blocks to make a row, alternating block placement; press seams toward Hourglass blocks. Repeat to make two rows.

2. Join the rows referring to the Placement Diagram to complete the pieced center; press seams in one direction.

3. Sew F, G, H and I strips to the pieced center in alphabetical order, referring to the Placement Diagram for positioning, pressing seams toward strips after each addition.

Completing the Runner

1. Sandwich the batting between the completed top and prepared backing; pin or baste layers together to hold.

2. Quilt as desired by hand or machine; remove pins or basting. Trim excess backing and batting even with runner top.

3. Join binding strips on short ends to make one long strip; press seams open. Fold the strip in half along length with wrong sides together; press.

4. Sew binding to right side of runner edges, mitering corners and overlapping ends. Fold binding to the back side and stitch in place to finish. ◈

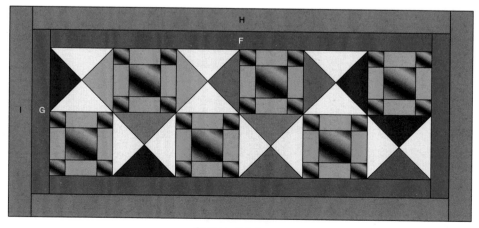

Colors of Autumn
Placement Diagram 53" x 25"

Diagonal Squares & Stripes

Design by Mary Ayres

Let the stripes in the fabric create the design on your next runner.

Project Specifications
Skill Level: Beginner
Runner Size: 48¾" x 20¼"

Materials
- 1 yard 45"-wide home decorator stripe (exact amount depends on width of stripe and the way the pattern is cut)
- 1⅓ yards coordinating home decorator stripe
- Batting 55" x 26"
- Backing 55" x 26"
- Neutral-color all-purpose thread
- Quilting thread
- 4½ yards coordinating cord edging
- Basic sewing tools and supplies

Cutting
1. Cut two 3½" x 43¼" C strips and two 3½" x 20¾" D strips along the length of the coordinating stripe.

2. Cut (21) 5½" x 5½" A squares from same section of wide stripe fabric.

3. Cut (12) 5½" x 5½" B squares from a different section of the wide stripe fabric.

Completing the Top
1. Arrange the A and B squares on a work surface, alternating stripes, referring to Figure 1. ***Note:*** *Place stripes that are cut from the same section going in the same direction.*

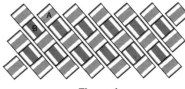

Figure 1

2. Join the A and B squares as arranged in rows, adding single squares at corners as necessary, again referring to Figure 1; press seams in adjacent rows in opposite directions.

3. Join the rows; press seams in one direction.

4. Trim excess from squares at edges, trimming ¼" from corners of B to square up edges as shown in Figure 2.

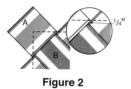

Figure 2

5. Sew C strips to opposite long sides and D strips to the short ends to complete the pieced top; press seams toward C and D strips.

Completing the Runner

1. Trim batting and backing the same size as the completed runner top; baste batting to the wrong side of the pieced top.

2. Sew cord edging around runner front ¼" from edges, beginning and ending in a corner.

3. Pin runner back right sides together with the front/batting piece; stitch all around, leaving a 5" opening on one side.

4. Trim seams at corners; trim batting close to stitching. Turn runner right side out through the opening; turn opening edges under ¼" and hand-stitch closed.

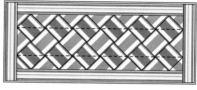

Figure 3

5. Machine-quilt along length through centers of squares, referring to Figure 3, along stripe lines on borders and close to seam at edges to finish. ◈

Diagonal Squares & Stripes
Placement Diagram 48¾" x 20¼"

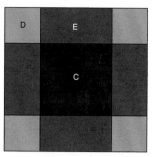

Uneven Nine-Patch
6" x 6" Block
Make 4

Country Garden

Design by Connie Kauffman

Create a flower garden for your table
with pretty floral prints.

Project Specifications
Skill Level: Beginner
Runner Size: 33" x 21"
Block Size: 6" x 6"
Number of Blocks: 4

Materials
- ¼ yard dark burgundy floral
- ¼ yard tan floral
- ¼ yard burgundy/peach print
- ¼ yard peach tonal
- ¼ yard green tonal
- Batting 39" x 27"
- Backing 39" x 27"
- Neutral-color all-purpose thread
- Quilting thread
- Basic sewing tools and supplies

Cutting
1. Cut one 6½" x 6½" A square dark burgundy floral with large motif centered.

2. Cut four 3½" x 3½" C squares from smaller floral sections of the dark burgundy floral.

3. Cut six 6½" x 6½" F squares tan floral with large motif centered in each square.

4. Cut two 3½" by fabric width strips burgundy/peach print; subcut strips into (30) 2" E rectangles.

5. Cut two 2" by fabric width strips peach tonal; subcut strips into (40) 2" B squares.

6. Cut one 3⅜" by fabric width strip green tonal; subcut strip into three 3⅜" squares. Cut each square on both diagonals to make 12 G triangles.

7. Cut two 2" by fabric width strips green tonal; subcut strips into (28) 2" B squares.

Completing the Blocks
1. To complete one Uneven Nine-Patch block, sew E to opposite sides of C; press seams toward C as shown in Figure 1.

Figure 1

2. Sew D to opposite ends of E; press seams toward E as shown in Figure 2. Repeat to make two D-E units.

Figure 2

3. Sew a D-E unit to opposite long sides of the C-E unit to complete one block; press seams toward the D-E units.

4. Repeat steps 1–3 to complete four Uneven Nine-Patch blocks.

Completing the Top
1. Mark a diagonal line from corner to corner on the wrong side of each B square.

2. Place a B square right sides together on each corner of A and stitch on the marked lines as shown in Figure 3; trim seams to ¼" and press B to the right side to complete one A-B unit, again referring to Figure 3.

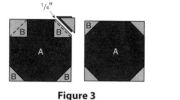

Figure 3   **Figure 4**

3. Repeat step 2 with B and F to complete six B-F units as shown in Figure 4.

4. Sew D to each end of E; press seams toward E. Repeat to make 10 D-E units.

5. Sew a D-E unit to one side of a B-F unit to make an end unit as shown in Figure 5; press seams toward the B-F unit. Repeat to make six end units.

Figure 5   **Figure 6**

6. Join two end units with one Uneven Nine-Patch block to make the top row as shown in Figure 6; press seams away from the end units. Repeat to make the bottom row.

7. Join the A-B unit with two Uneven Nine-Patch blocks and two end units to make the center row as shown in Figure 7; press seams toward the Uneven Nine-Patch blocks.

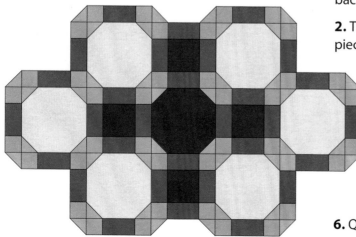

Country Garden
Placement Diagram 33" x 21"

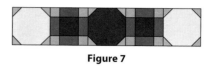

Figure 7

8. Sew G to each end of a D-E unit as shown in Figure 8; press seams toward G. Repeat to make four D-E-G units.

Figure 8   **Figure 9**

9. Sew D to one end of E and add G to make a G-D-E unit as shown in Figure 9; press seams toward E and G; repeat to make two units and two reverse units, again referring to Figure 9.

10. Sew two D-E-G units and one each G-D-E unit and reverse G-D-E unit to the top and bottom rows referring to Figure 10; press seams away from the rows.

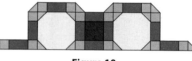

Figure 10

11. Sew a D-E-G unit to each end of the center row; press seams toward the D-E-G units.

12. Sew the top and bottom rows to the center row to complete the pieced top; press seams away from the center row.

Completing the Runner

1. Place backing piece right side up on batting; place completed top right sides together with backing; pin edges.

2. Trim backing and batting even with the pieced top.

3. Sew all around, leaving a 4" opening along one side; clip inner corners. Trim batting close to stitching.

4. Turn right side out through opening; press edges flat.

5. Turn opening edges to the inside; hand-stitch opening closed.

6. Quilt as desired by hand or machine to finish. ◈

Seeing Circles

Design by Connie Kauffman

Create a contemporary look with simple appliquéd circles.

- -

Project Specifications
Skill Level: Beginner
Runner Size: 37" x 13½"

Materials
- ⅓ yard blue tonal
- ⅓ yard brown mottled
- ½ yard aqua/brown print
- Batting 40" x 17"
- Backing 40" x 17"
- All-purpose thread to match fabrics
- Quilting thread
- ½ yard fusible web
- ⅓ yard fabric stabilizer
- Basic sewing tools and supplies

Cutting
1. Cut one 10½" by fabric width strip aqua/brown print; subcut strip into three 10½" A squares.

2. Cut three 2¼" by fabric width strips brown mottled; subcut strips into six 10½" B strips and four 14" C strips.

3. Prepare full-size circle pattern using template on page 173. Trace two circle shapes onto the paper side of the fusible web; cut out shapes, leaving a margin around each shape.

4. Fuse shapes to the wrong side of fabric as directed on pattern; cut out shapes on traced lines. Remove paper backing.

Completing the Top
1. Sew a B strip to opposite sides of each A square; press seams toward B strips.

2. Join the A-B units with C strips to complete the pieced top.

3. Arrange and fuse the circles on the pieced top referring to the Placement Diagram for positioning.

4. Cut two 8" x 8" squares fabric stabilizer; pin a square behind each fused circle.

5. Using thread to match fabric and a machine buttonhole stitch, sew around the inner and outer edges of each circle shape; when stitching is complete, remove fabric stabilizer.

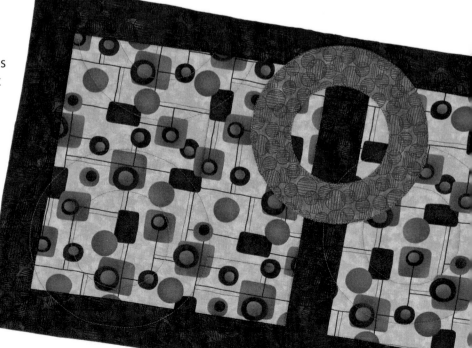

Completing the Runner

1. Place backing piece right side up on batting; place completed top right sides together with backing; pin edges.

2. Trim backing and batting even with the pieced top.

3. Sew all around, leaving a 4" opening along one side; clip outer corners. Trim batting close to stitching.

4. Turn right side out through opening; press edges flat.

5. Turn opening edges to the inside; hand-stitch opening closed.

6. Quilt as desired by hand or machine to finish. ◈

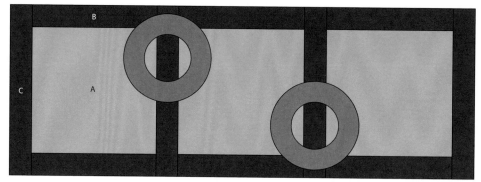

Seeing Circles
Placement Diagram 37" x 13½"

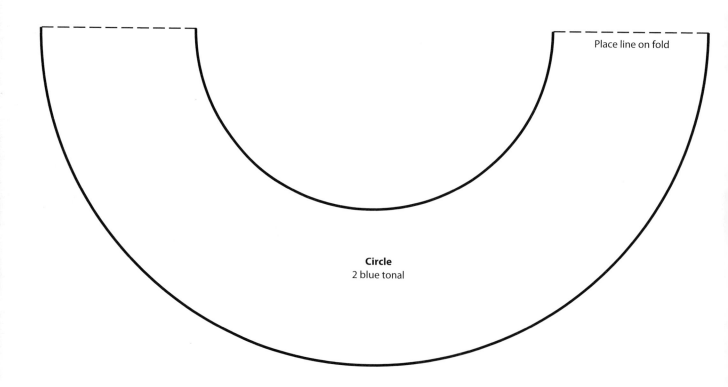

Place line on fold

Circle
2 blue tonal

Poinsettia Table Runner

Design by BrendaBarb Designs/Brenda Connelly and Barb Miller

A simple pieced runner base is elegant with just a bit of appliqué in the center.

Project Specifications
Skill Level: Beginner
Runner Size: 40" x 18" without prairie points

Materials
- 1 (4" x 4") scrap gold
- 5 (6" x 12") red scraps from very dark burgundy to light red-orange
- 2 (6" x 12") scraps contrasting greens
- 1 (1½" x 12") J strip green tonal
- ⅝ yard white tonal
- ¾ yard gold metallic tonal
- Batting 43" x 21"
- Backing 43" x 21"
- Neutral-color all-purpose thread
- Invisible thread
- Quilting thread
- ½ yard 12"-wide lightweight double-stick fusible web
- ½ yard fabric stabilizer
- 1 each brown, black and dark green permanent fabric markers
- Appliqué pressing sheet
- Basic sewing tools and supplies

Cutting
1. Cut one 12½" by fabric width strip white tonal; subcut into one 12½" A square and four 2½" x 18½" F strips.

2. Cut one 1½" by fabric width C strip white tonal.

3. Cut one 2" by fabric width strip white tonal; subcut strip into eight 4½" G pieces.

4. Cut one 1½" by fabric width B strip gold metallic tonal.

5. Cut two 2½" by fabric width strips gold metallic tonal; subcut strips into two 14½" D strips and two 18½" E strips.

6. Cut two 2" by fabric width strips gold metallic tonal; subcut strip into (12) 4½" H pieces.

7. Cut one 2½" by fabric width I strip gold metallic tonal; subcut into two 12" I pieces.

8. Cut one 3½" by fabric width strip gold metallic tonal; subcut strip into two 18½" K strips.

9. Cut two 2½" by fabric width strips gold metallic tonal; subcut strips into (18) 2½" L squares.

Completing the Pieced Top
1. Sew the B strip to the C strip with right sides together along length to make a B-C strip set; press seams toward B.

2. Subcut the B-C strip set into (26) 1½" B-C units as shown in Figure 1.

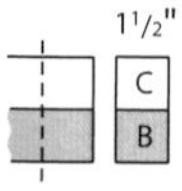

Figure 1

3. Join six B-C units end to end to make a B-C strip as shown in Figure 2; press seams in one direction. Repeat to make two B-C strips.

Figure 2

4. Sew a B-C strip to opposite sides of A as shown in Figure 3; press seams toward A.

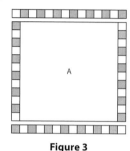

Figure 3

5. Join seven B-C units end to end to make a longer B-C strip; press seams in one direction. Repeat to make two longer B-C strips.

6. Sew the longer B-C strips to the top and bottom of A, again referring to Figure 3; press seams toward A.

7. Sew D to opposite sides and E to the top and bottom of the A-B-C unit to complete the pieced center; press seams toward D and E.

8. Sew the J strip between the two I strips with right sides together along length; press seams toward J.

9. Subcut the I-J strip set into six 1½" I-J units as shown in Figure 4.

Figure 4

10. Sew H to opposite sides of an I-J unit to complete an H-I-J unit as shown in Figure 5; press seams toward H pieces. Repeat to make six H-I-J units.

Figure 5

11. Join three H-I-J units with four G pieces to make a pieced row as shown in Figure 6; press seams away from G. Repeat to make two pieced rows.

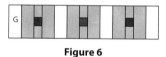

Figure 6

12. Sew an F strip to opposite sides of each pieced row; add K to one side to complete an end unit as shown in Figure 7; press seams toward F and K.

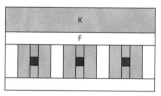

Figure 7

13. Sew an end unit to the center unit to complete the pieced top; press seams toward the center unit.

Completing the Appliqué

1. Trace the appliqué shapes onto the paper side of the fusible web as directed on patterns; cut out shapes, leaving a margin around each one.

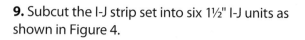

2. Fuse shapes to the wrong side of fabrics as directed on patterns for color; cut out shapes on traced lines. Remove paper backing.

3. Referring to the instructions with the appliqué pressing sheet and using the full-size motifs given, create one large and two small poinsettia motifs, layering pieces in numerical order.

4. Arrange the motifs with leaves on the pieced center referring to the Placement Diagram and project photo for positioning; when satisfied with placement, fuse shapes in place.

5. Cut one 16" x 16" square fabric stabilizer; pin to the wrong side of the center A area of the pieced top.

6. Using invisible thread, machine buttonhole-stitch around each fused shape; remove fabric stabilizer.

7. Add vines, leaf and flower-center details as marked on pattern using permanent fabric markers in appropriate colors to complete the runner top.

Completing the Runner

1. Fold each L square in half and in half again to create a prairie point triangle as shown in Figure 8.

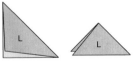

Figure 8

2. Pin one L prairie point in the center and at each end of each K strip on the runner ends as shown in Figure 9.

Figure 9

3. Arrange and pin three more L prairie points between the center and the each end as shown in Figure 10, overlapping prairie points as necessary to fit edge; when satisfied with positioning, machine-baste in place ⅛" from edge.

Figure 10

4. Place backing piece right side up on batting; place completed top right sides together with backing; pin edges.

5. Trim backing and batting even with the pieced top.

6. Sew all around, leaving a 6" opening along one side; clip inner corners. Trim batting close to stitching.

7. Turn right side out through opening; press edges flat.

8. Turn opening edges to the inside; hand-stitch opening closed.

9. Quilt as desired by hand or machine to finish. ◈

Poinsettia Table Runner
Placement Diagram 40" x 18" without prairie points

Leaf
Cut 3
green
scraps

Large Poinsettia Motif
Cut 1 each petal red scraps
Cut 1 center gold scrap

Top

Small Poinsettia Motif B
Cut 1 each petal red scraps
Cut 1 each leaf green scrap
Cut 1 center gold scrap

Small Poinsettia Motif A
Cut 1 each petal red scraps
Cut 1 each leaf green scrap
Cut 1 center gold scrap

Try a New Technique

If you are ready to learn something new about quilting, these runners are ready and waiting. Learn to create a vintage look, make a reversible runner, use wool, try sashiko stitching, work with fabric strips and more.

Autumn Quartet

Design by Susan Fletcher

Wool makes the perfect runner
for this design with a folk-art flavor.

Project Specifications
Skill Level: Beginner
Runner Size: 52" x 11"

Materials
- 52" x 11" rectangle green wool for background
- Scraps orange, rust, gold, and bright and dark green wool
- Backing 53½" x 13"
- All-purpose thread to match backing
- Embroidery thread to match and contrast with appliqué shapes
- Basic sewing tools and supplies

Cutting
1. Cut appliqué shapes as directed using patterns given. *Note: Use leaf patterns given as a guide; vary size and shapes to create diversity in design. Alternate use of bright and dark green in leaves with some having a dark base with bright layered top leaf and vice versa.*

Completing the Top
1. Fold the 52" x 11" wool rectangle along length and crease to mark the center.

2. Mark a point 8½" down on each side on each end.

Figure 1

3. Connect the marks on the sides with the creased centerline at each end and cut along these line to make pointed ends as shown in Figure 1.

4. Arrange and pin all appliqué shapes onto the background using the Placement Diagram and project photo as guides.

5. Hand-stitch pieces in place using a buttonhole stitch and 2 strands of matching or contrasting embroidery floss.

6. Use a thorn stitch and contrasting embroidery floss to add tail feathers to birds as shown in stitch drawing and referring to bird pattern for positioning.

7. Add French knots on birds' wings using contrasting embroidery floss; repeat for eyes on birds.

8. Use a combination of thorn, outline and running stitches on leaves to complete the runner top.

Completing the Runner
1. Center the completed runner top on the backing piece; trim backing edges ¾" wider than runner.

2. Turn backing edges in ¼" all around and press.

3. Center the completed runner top on the pressed backing piece again; fold the backing edges to the right side of the runner and hand-stitch in place all around to finish. ◈

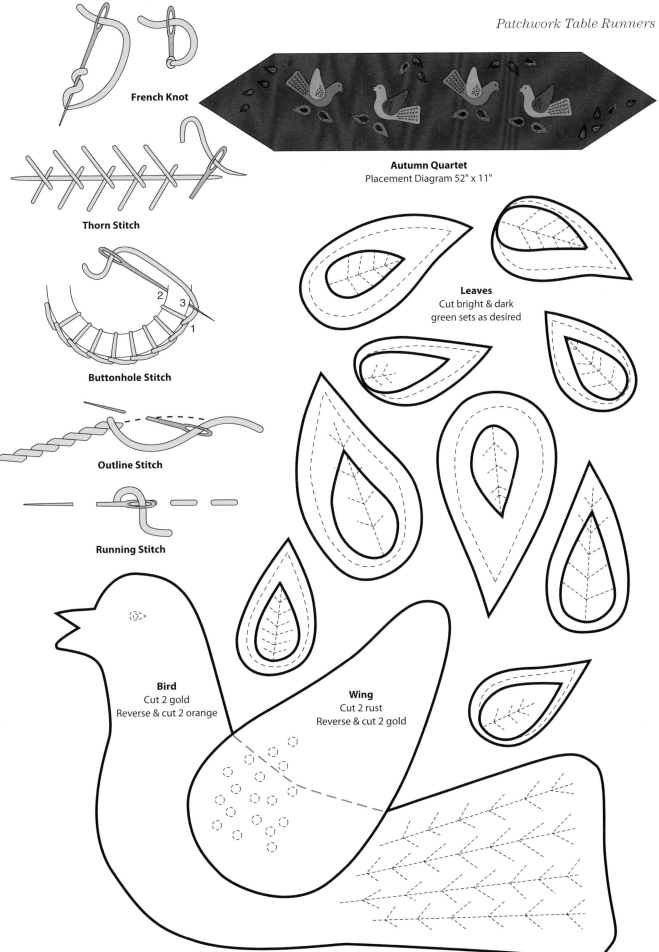

French Knot

Thorn Stitch

Buttonhole Stitch

Outline Stitch

Running Stitch

Autumn Quartet
Placement Diagram 52" x 11"

Leaves
Cut bright & dark
green sets as desired

Bird
Cut 2 gold
Reverse & cut 2 orange

Wing
Cut 2 rust
Reverse & cut 2 gold

105

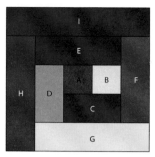

Side 1 Log Cabin A
5" x 5" Block
Make 4

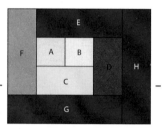

Side 1 Log Cabin B
5" x 4" Block
Make 4

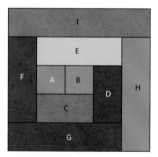

Side 2 Log Cabin A
5" x 5" Block
Make 4

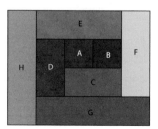

Side 2 Log Cabin B
5" x 4" Block
Make 4

Reversible Log Cabin Runner

Design by Christine Schultz

Make a two-in-one runner in two different color schemes.

Project Notes

This project is pieced and quilted at the same time. Flannel instead of batting is sandwiched between side 1 and side 2 strips and stitched together as one. This process creates a reversible runner that finishes up quickly.

The binding is also reversible when made with two narrow seamed strips. The seam is right on the edge of the runner so that each side has its own matching binding.

Project Specifications

Skill Level: Beginner
Runner Size:
   26½" x 13½"

Block Size: 5" x 5" and 5" x 4"
Number of Blocks: 4 and 4 for each side

Materials

- ¼ yard binding fabric for each side
- ⅓ yard border fabric for each side
- ¾ yard total assorted coordinating prints or scraps for each side
- ¾ yard neutral-color flannel for filler
- Neutral-color all-purpose thread
- Quilting thread
- Basic sewing tools and supplies

Cutting

1. Select coordinating prints or scraps for side 1 of the runner. Cut four 1½"-wide pieces for each letter in lengths as follows: 1½" A and B; 2½" C and D; 3½" E and F; 4½" G and H; and 5½" I. Cut three 1½" x 10½" J strips.

2. Repeat step 1 with coordinating prints or scraps for side 2 of the runner. Repeat with flannel to cut two each letter A–I and three J.

3. Cut two 2¼" x 23½" K strips and two 2¼" x 14" L strips from each coordinating border fabric. Repeat with flannel.

4. Cut three 1¼" by fabric width strips from each binding fabric.

Completing the Blocks

1. To piece one reversible A block, select one each side 1 A and B squares and side 2 A and B squares, and one each flannel A and B squares. Stack from bottom to top as follows: side 2 B right side up, side 2 A right side down, flannel A, side 1 A right side up, side 1 B right side down and flannel B on top.

2. Stitch a ¼" seam on one edge of the stack; fold the bottom side 2 B square out away from the stack as shown in Figure 1. Fold the top flannel and side 1 B squares over the top of the side 2 B square, again referring to Figure 1; press toward the side B pieces to complete the A-B unit. The seam allowance will be enclosed in the B side of the unit as shown in the side view in Figure 1.

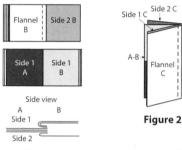

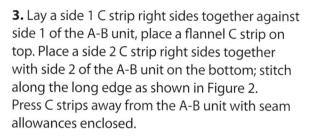

Figure 1

Figure 2

3. Lay a side 1 C strip right sides together against side 1 of the A-B unit, place a flannel C strip on top. Place a side 2 C strip right sides together with side 2 of the A-B unit on the bottom; stitch along the long edge as shown in Figure 2. Press C strips away from the A-B unit with seam allowances enclosed.

4. Continue adding strips in alphabetical order around the center in the same manner, always pressing the last strips added away from the center unit. **Note:** *When layering strips, the flannel strips will always be on the top, and the side 1 and side 2 strips will always be right sides together with their respective sides.* Complete four each reversible A and B blocks, referring to the block drawings for strip placement.

Completing the Top

1. Sew sides 1 and 2 I strips and a flannel I strip to each B block in the same manner used to complete the blocks; press I strips away from the blocks.

2. Fold back the side 1 I strip and sew an A block to the B block with side 2 of blocks right sides together and through all layers as shown in Figure 3.

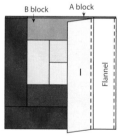

Figure 3

3. Fold the A block out from the B block. Fold the raw edge of the loose I strip under ¼"; press the I strip over the exposed flannel and the raw edge of the A block so the folded edge meets the seam line as shown in Figure 4; hand-stitch in place to complete a two-block row. Repeat to make three more rows.

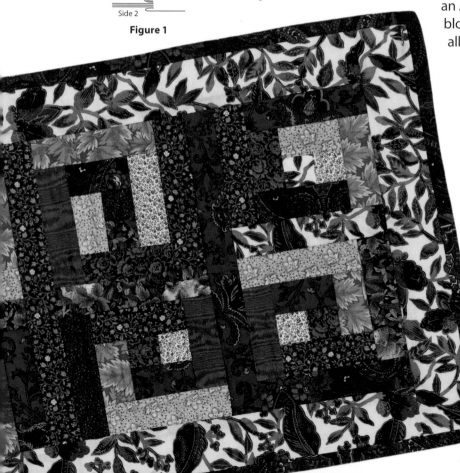

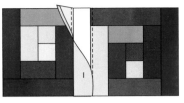

Figure 4

4. Sew the rows together with the J pieces as in steps 2 and 3 as shown in Figure 5.

Figure 5

5. Add the K and L border strips using the same method to complete the reversible pieced top.

Completing the Runner

1. Join same-fabric binding strips on short ends to make one long strip each fabric; press seams open.

2. Join the two stitched binding strips with right sides together along one long side; press seam open.

3. Sew side 1 binding to side 1 runner edges, mitering corners and overlapping ends. Fold side 2 binding to side 2 and hand-stitch in place to finish. ◈

Side 1 Reversible Log Cabin
Placement Diagram 26½" x 13½"

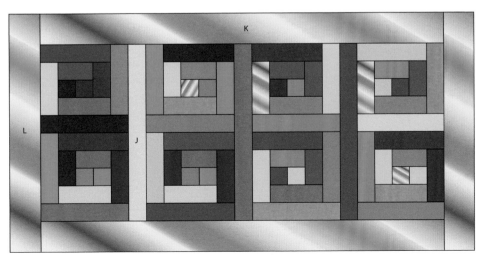

Side 2 Reversible Log Cabin
Placement Diagram 26½" x 13½"

Coiled-Strip Runner

Design by Connie Kauffman

Use up leftover Jelly Roll strips in this little runner reminiscent of a braided rug.

Project Specifications
Skill Level: Beginner
Runner Size: 17½" x 14"

Materials
- 14 (2½" by fabric width) strips
- Neutral-color all-purpose thread
- 25–30 feet 5mm macramé cord
- Spring clothespin
- Basic sewing tools and supplies

Cutting
1. Cut each 2½"-wide strip in half across width to make two lengths. Cut each length in half along length to make two 1¼"-wide strips.

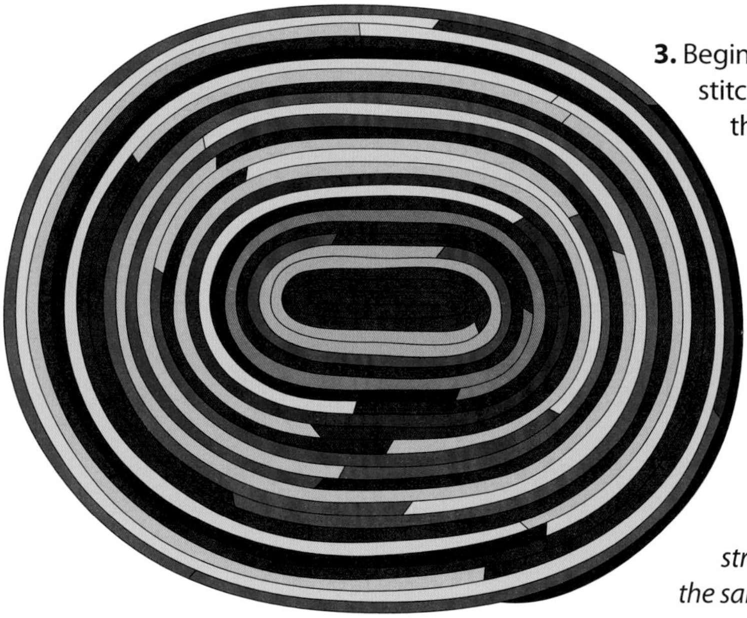

Completing the Runner
1. Wrap a fabric strip tightly around the cord as shown in Figure 1; continue until about 9" of cord is covered and clip with the clothespin to hold the fabric and cord together. ***Note:*** *Jelly Roll strips will have a straight edge and a serrated edge when cut. Be consistent and keep only the straight side exposed.*

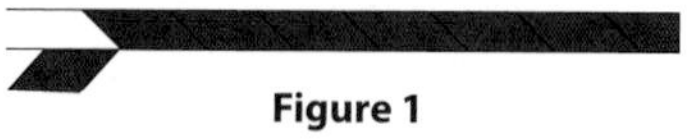

Figure 1

2. Fold the fabric end down, and fold 4" of cord against itself as shown in Figure 2.

4"

Figure 2

3. Begin sewing a zigzag stitch (wide enough stitch that the needle catches both sides) at the turned end of the wrapped cord as shown in Figure 3. Stop with the needle down and continue to wrap fabric around cord for several inches, using clothespin to hold.

Figure 3

4. Hold the wrapped coil around the first sewn coils and zigzag between coils. Continue this process, adding new fabrics as needed. ***Note:*** *Each new strip is just overlapped and wrapped in the same process.*

Coiled-Strip Runner
Placement Diagram 17½" x 14"

5. When the strips are used up, or the runner is the size you want, cut the cord diagonally and continue to wrap the fabric around itself for 1"–2".

6. Hold wrapped end and zigzag as before; backstitch to secure end threads.

7. Trim all loose and frayed threads when runner is complete. ◈

Tip

Make your own Jelly Roll strips by cutting scraps of coordinating fabrics into 1¼" strips. For this project, the length of the strips can vary, making it a great way to use up scraps.

~Connie Kauffman

Vintage Linen Runner

Design by Mary Ayres

Vintage linens create a romantic runner.

Project Notes

Use the perfect parts of vintage linens, cutting away stains or damaged areas. Add an 8"–10" square or round doily cut in half for the ends.

Project Specifications

Skill Level: Beginner
Runner Size: 51" x 17" (without end triangles)

Materials

- Pieces of vintage linens to coordinate with pink and blue fabrics
- 8"–10" square or round doily for ends
- ⅛ yard light blue dot
- ½ yard light pink dot
- ½ yard light blue solid
- Batting 57" x 23"
- Backing 57" x 23"
- All-purpose thread to match linens
- Quilting thread

Cutting

1. Cut one 11½" by fabric width strip light blue solid; subcut strip into four 9½" A rectangles.

2. Cut four 3½" by fabric width strips light pink dot; subcut strips into five 11½" B strips and eight 9½" C strips.

3. Cut one 3½" by fabric width strip light blue dot; subcut strip into (10) 3½" D squares.

Completing the Top

1. Cut vintage linens and doilies to make usable parts.

2. Place cut pieces on top of A rectangles, overlapping as desired, leaving spaces between them for the A pieces to show through. When satisfied with the arrangement, pin, then baste in place.

3. Trim edges of linens even with A.

4. Hand-stitch linen pieces in place using a blind stitch.

5. Arrange and join four vintage A rectangles with five B strips; press seams toward B.

6. Join four C strips with five D squares to make a side border strip; press seams toward C. Repeat to make two side border strips.

7. Sew a side border strip to opposite sides of the A-B center to complete the pieced top.

Completing the Runner

1. Cut the 8"–10" square doily in half on one diagonal to make two E triangles, or cut a round doily in half to make two E half circles.

2. Pin one E piece to each end of the pieced top as shown in Figure 1; baste to hold.

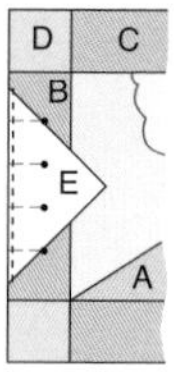

Figure 1

3. Layer batting, backing right side up and runner right side down; pin edges. Trim batting and backing even with the pieced top.

4. Sew all around, leaving a 4" opening along one side; trim batting and backing close to runner edges. Clip inner corners.

5. Turn right side out through opening; press edges flat.

6. Turn opening edges to the inside; hand-stitch closed.

7. Quilt as desired by hand or machine to finish. ◈

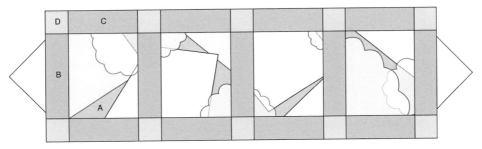

Vintage Linen Runner
Placement Diagram 51" x 17"

Floating Blossoms

Design by Susan Fletcher

One simple stitching pattern creates a striking design when used to make a table runner using sashiko, the traditional Japanese embroidery.

Project Specifications
Skill Level: Beginner
Runner Size: 42½" x 10¼"

Materials
- 2 (10¾" x 43") rectangles navy blue solid
- Backing 10¾" x 43"
- All-purpose thread to match fabric
- White No. 5 pearl cotton
- Permanent marking pen
- 10¾" x 43" lightweight fusible interfacing
- Basic sewing tools and supplies

Completing the Top
1. Fold the 10¾" x 43" rectangle of lightweight fusible interfacing in half with right sides together along the length and crease to mark the center.

2. Measure and mark 7¼" down from the corner on the raw edge; draw a line from the mark to the folded edge as shown in Figure 1. Cut along the marked line; repeat on opposite end.

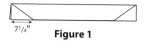

7¼"   **Figure 1**

3. Draw a line along the creased center.

4. Tape the fusible interfacing rectangle to a table surface with fusible side down; using a permanent marking pen, draw a line ⅜" inside the cut edge of the interfacing all the way around to mark the sewing line. Draw a second line ¼" inside the first line to make the sashiko stitching line.

5. Trace the floating blossom design given onto paper, including center and diagonal guidelines.

6. Slide the tracing under the interfacing and position it so that the first blossom petal begins about ½" from the marked stitching line at runner point as shown in Figure 2. ***Note:*** *Be sure the center guideline of the pattern is aligned with the one you drew on the interfacing.* Trace blossoms and diagonal guidelines onto the interfacing, moving the design as necessary.

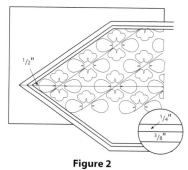

½"   ¼"   ⅜"

Figure 2

7. Untape the interfacing and lay it, fusible side down, onto the wrong side of one fabric rectangle, aligning along edges; fuse the interfacing to the fabric. ***Note:*** *Begin at the center and work toward the ends. Lift, rather than slide, the iron so the design does not get distorted.*

8. Trim ends of fabric to match interfacing.

Stitching Sashiko

Note: *You will be stitching from the wrong side of the runner top. Make the stitches on the interfacing side shorter than those that will show on the fabric side. Begin and end all stitching on the interfacing side.*

1. Refer to Figure 3 to begin stitching; using white pearl cotton, insert the needle through the interfacing to the fabric side on a design line, leaving a 1" tail on the interfacing side. Move the needle ¼" along the design and bring it back to the interfacing side. Move ⅛" along the design and go through to the fabric side. Come back up ¼" along the line; make one more stitch. Slide the needle through the previous stitches on the interfacing side and then back down to the fabric side ⅛" from the starting point. Pull stitches tight to secure thread end of pearl cotton, but do not gather.

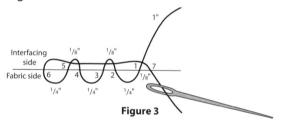

Figure 3

2. Continue stitching using a running stitch until you are near the end of the pearl cotton, then pass the needle under a few stitches on the interfacing side to secure the end of the pearl cotton.

3. When you need a new length of pearl cotton, begin by passing the needle under two or three stitches on the interfacing side.

4. When blossom stitching is complete, stitch on marked ¼" line around edge of runner.

Completing the Runner

1. Place backing piece right side up on batting; place completed top right sides together with backing; pin edges.

2. Trim backing and batting even with the pieced top.

Sashiko Tips

• *The stitch length is up to you. You will soon find your own rhythm in stitching and the project will move along quickly and comfortably, but a rule of thumb is 4 stitches per inch on the front side of the design.*

• *Do not use a hoop when stitching; instead gather the fabric in your hand, sit in a comfortable chair and relax while you stitch.*

• *Put several stitches on the needle at a time, rather than taking one stitch at a time. Your stitching will be faster and smoother.*

• *Don't cut the thread between blossoms; instead, carry it across the back of the fabric to the next blossom. When you do this, and whenever you move from one petal to another on the blossoms, be sure to leave a little slack in the thread on the back of the fabric to prevent puckering.*

• *Check frequently at first that your stitches are not pulling on the front of the fabric, especially anywhere you have turned a corner or crossed a space.*

3. Sew all around, leaving a 4" opening along one side; clip inner corners. Trim batting close to stitching.

4. Turn right side out through opening; press edges flat.

5. Turn opening edges to the inside; hand-stitch opening closed.

6. Quilt as desired by hand or machine to finish. ◈

Floating Blossoms
Placement Diagram 42½" x 10¼"

Floating Blossoms Design

Always match the centerline, a diagonal line and an intersection of the centerline and a diagonal line when you are moving and tracing the design onto the fusible interfacing. Use the lines as guides for spacing, not the blossoms. The blossom spacing is not identical. This increases the sense that they are floating. When tracing partial blossoms, it may help to find a blossom that matches the one you are completing.

Running Stitch

Pink Posy Runner, Napkin & Napkin Ring

Design by Chris Malone

Embroidered flowers create floral bouquets in the pieced baskets of this pretty summertime table set.

Project Notes

Instructions are given to make one napkin and napkin ring. You will need additional fabric to make multiple napkins and napkin rings—one 17½" square each light and dark prints, and one elastic strip for each napkin and ring.

Project Specifications

Skill Level: Intermediate
Runner Size: 36" x 12" without yo-yos and leaves
Napkin Size: 17" x 17"
Napkin Ring: 5" x 2¼"

Materials

- 1 fat quarter each pink and red prints for napkin
- ⅛ yard each 5 assorted light to dark pink and red prints
- ⅓ yard dark pink print
- ½ yard white tonal
- ½ yard green print
- Batting 42" x 18"
- Backing 42" x 18"
- Fleece or lightweight batting scraps for leaves
- All-purpose thread to match fabrics
- Quilting thread
- Red, pink and green embroidery floss
- 6 (⅝") red buttons
- 1 (⅞") red button
- 5½" length ¾"-wide elastic
- Air-soluble marking pen
- No-fray solution
- Basic sewing tools and supplies

Cutting

1. Prepare templates for pieces A–G using patterns given; cut as directed on each piece. Prepare pattern and cut yo-yo circles as directed.

2. Cut 16 assorted 3½" x 3½" J squares light to dark pink and red prints.

3. Cut one each 17½" x 17½" square pink and red print for napkin.

4. Cut four 2½" x 4½" H pieces white tonal.

5. Cut two 7½" x 12½" I pieces white tonal.

6. Cut two 1½" x 12½" L pieces green print

7. Cut one 2⅜" x 9½" K strip green print for each napkin holder.

8. Cut three 2¼" by fabric width strips green print for binding.

Runner

Completing the Basket Bases

1. Sew D to one side of C as shown in Figure 1; press seam toward D.

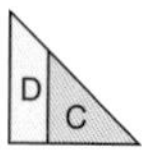

Figure 1

2. Continue to add E–G pieces to the C-D unit in alphabetical order as shown in Figure 2, press seams toward the most recently added strips before adding subsequent strips.

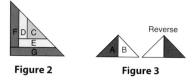

Figure 2   **Figure 3**

3. Sew A to B as shown in Figure 3; press seam toward A. Repeat to make a reverse A-B unit, again referring to Figure 3.

4. Sew the A-B and reverse A-B units to the F and G sides of the pieced unit to complete a basket-base unit as shown in Figure 4; press seams toward the A-B units.

Figure 4   **Figure 5**

5. Repeat steps 1–4 to complete two basket-base units.

Completing the Top

1. Sew H to opposite short sides of each basket-base unit as shown in Figure 5; press seams toward H pieces.

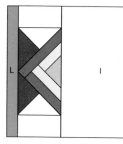

Figure 6   **Figure 7**

2. Sew L to the A side and I to the C side of each basket-base unit as shown in Figure 6; press seams toward I and L.

3. Using the air-soluble marking pen, transfer the embroidery design to each I piece, aligning the edge of the design with the edge of the basket base as shown in Figure 7.

4. Use 2 strands of floss and an outline or stem stitch to embroider the red basket handles, pink flowers, and green stems and leaves.

5. Join four J squares to make a row; repeat to make four rows, arranging squares in rows to avoid same-fabric squares touching; press seams in opposite directions in adjacent rows.

6. Join the J rows to complete the pieced J unit; press seams in one direction.

7. Sew an embroidered unit to each end of the J unit to complete the pieced top; press seams away from the J unit.

Completing the Runner

1. Sandwich the batting between the completed top and prepared backing; pin or baste layers together.

2. Quilt as desired by hand or machine; remove pins or basting. Trim excess backing and batting even with runner top.

3. Join binding strips on short ends to make one long strip; press seams open. Fold the strip in half along length with wrong sides together; press.

4. Sew binding to the right side of the runner edges, mitering corners and overlapping ends. Fold binding to the back side and stitch in place.

5. Sew a ⅝" red button to the center of each embroidered flower, stitching through all layers.

6. To make yo-yo flowers, finger-press a ⅛" hem around the outer edge of each fabric circle; hand-baste in place using a generous ¼" long stitch length. Pull the thread to draw up the edges into a tight circle to make a yo-yo flower as shown in Figure 8; knot the thread and clip. Repeat to make 10 yo-yo flowers.

Figure 8

7. Hand-stitch five yo-yo flowers to each short end of the runner referring to the Placement Diagram for positioning.

8. Trace the leaf pattern eight times on the wrong side of the green print, leaving at least a ½" margin between each shape.

9. Fold the fabric in half with right sides together with the traced patterns on top; pin to fleece or lightweight batting.

10. Sew all around on traced lines as shown in Figure 9; cut out ⅛" from seam. Trim fleece close to stitch and clip curves.

Figure 9

11. Cut a slash through one layer of fabric only; apply no-fray solution to the cut edges and let dry.

12. Turn right side out through opening; press edges flat.

13. Whipstitch the edges of the opening closed.

14. Machine-stitch through the center of each leaf to make vein.

15. Attach two leaves to each corner of the runner by placing the leaves under the edges of the flowers and tacking them to the underside of the flower and to the edge of the binding as shown in Figure 10 to finish.

Figure 10

Napkin

1. Pin two 17½" x 17½" napkin squares right sides together; sew all around using a ¼" seam allowance, leaving a 3" opening on one side.

2. Trim corners; turn right side out through opening and press edges flat.

3. Fold seam allowance in at opening; hand-stitch opening closed.

4. Topstitch ¼" from edge all around.

Napkin Ring

1. Prepare one yo-yo flower and two leaves as for runner. Sew a ⅞" red button to the center of the flower.

2. Fold the K strip in half along length with right sides together; stitch ¼" from the long edges. Press seam open and turn right side out; center seam on the back of the tube and press as shown in Figure 11.

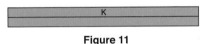

Figure 11

3. Insert the piece of elastic into the tube, gathering the tube on the elastic so the ends are even with the tube raw edges as shown in Figure 12; pin to hold.

Figure 12   **Figure 13**

4. Fold the tube in half with seamed side inside and stitch the short ends together as shown in Figure 13; press seam open.

5. Tack a leaf to each seam allowance edge of the ring; tack the flower over the seam to complete the napkin ring. ◈

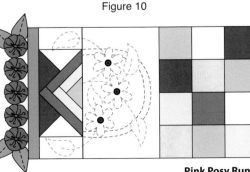

Pink Posy Runner
Placement Diagram 36" x 12" without yo-yos & leaves

Pink Posy Napkin Ring & Napkin
Placement Diagram
17" x 17" napkin
5" x 2¼" ring

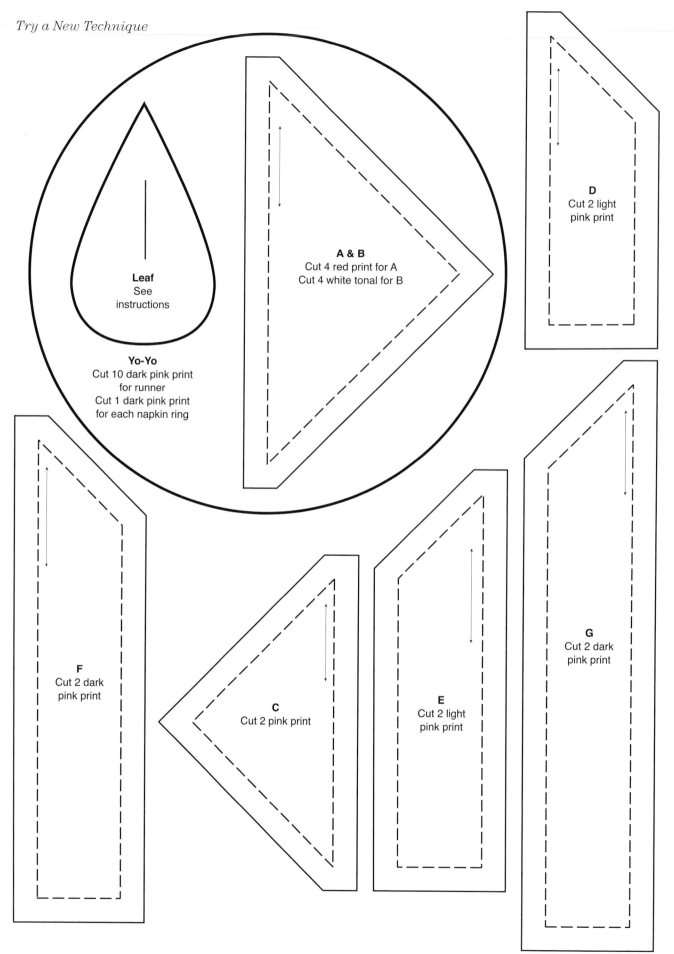

Leaf
See
instructions

Yo-Yo
Cut 10 dark pink print
for runner
Cut 1 dark pink print
for each napkin ring

A & B
Cut 4 red print for A
Cut 4 white tonal for B

D
Cut 2 light
pink print

F
Cut 2 dark
pink print

C
Cut 2 pink print

E
Cut 2 light
pink print

G
Cut 2 dark
pink print

Embroidery Pattern
Align with center of basket base
Enlarge 125%

Vintage Hearts & Crazy Patches

Design by Jodi Warner

Paper-piecing, crazy patchwork and lace create a vintage look in a beautiful table runner.

Project Specifications
Skill Level: Advanced
Runner Size: 42¼" x 14¼"

Materials
- Scraps 12 assorted rose and blue prints, stripes and wovens
- Fat quarter cream mini-floral
- Fat quarter slate blue print
- ⅛ yard burgundy mottled
- ⅓ yard pale pink stripe
- ⅓ yard deep rose tonal
- ½ yard tan tonal
- ⅔ yard navy print
- Thin batting 48" x 20"
- Backing 48" x 20"
- All-purpose thread to match fabrics
- Quilting thread
- 1 yard 1¾"-wide cream flat lace
- 2 small-to-medium size coordinating tassels with attached cord
- Basic sewing tools and supplies

Cutting
1. Prepare templates for pieces A–D, K, L and N pieces; cut as directed on each piece. Transfer corner dots for inset seams.

2. Cut one 2" by fabric width strip slate blue print; subcut strip into (20) 2" squares for prairie points.

3. Cut one 1" by fabric width strip tan tonal; subcut strip into two 6½" I and two 7½" J strips.

4. Cut two 2" x 28" M strips navy print.

5. Cut remaining navy print into 2½"-wide bias strips to total 120" for binding.

6. Cut (12) 4" lengths and four 3" lengths burgundy mottled bias strips for spaghetti trim.

7. Make three copies each E, F, G and H paper-piecing patterns. Cut up one copy to make templates for each numbered piece. Cut fabric pieces from all remaining fabrics except navy print, cream mini-floral and tan tonal using templates, adding a ¼" seam allowance all around each piece and placing patterns printed side up on the wrong side of fabrics when cutting; keep pieces for each pattern together in envelopes to keep them from being mixed up later.

Completing the Fan Units
1. To make one fan unit, join eight A pieces as shown in Figure 1; press seams in one direction.

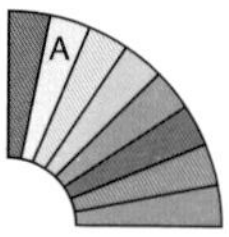

Figure 1

2. Center and sew B and C to the A unit as shown in Figure 2 to complete one fan unit, matching seams of the A unit to the dots on B and C; press seams toward B and away from C.

Figure 2

3. Repeat steps 1 and 2 to make two fan units.

4. Sew an I strip to one B edge and J to the remaining B edge of each unit as shown in Figure 3.

Figure 3

Completing the Paper-Pieced Units

1. Set stitch length to 18–20 stitches per inch; change needle to size 90—the larger needle will help perforate the paper and make paper removal easier.

2. Select one copy of E and previously cut fabric patches for E. Lay piece 1 right side up over space 1 on the unprinted side of the paper pattern, with one longer raw edge of piece 1 extending ¼" beyond the seam line between pieces 1 and 2 as shown in Figure 4.

Figure 4

3. Pin piece 2 right sides together with piece 1 along the ½" seam line.

4. Flip pinned paper pattern over and sew on the line between spaces 1 and 2, extending stitches slightly beyond both ends as shown in Figure 5. Clip threads and press piece 2 to the right side; check to be sure spaces 1 and 2 are completely covered before adding piece 3.

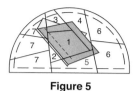

Figure 5

5. Continue adding pieces in numerical order until the paper pattern is complete; press without steam.

6. For sections with multiple pieces with the same number, such as sections 6 and 7, join the pieces to make a strip as shown in Figure 6. Press seams in one direction. Use the pieced strip as the piece to stitch to the paper pattern as shown in Figure 7.

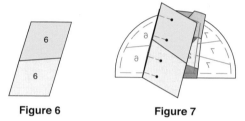

Figure 6　　　　**Figure 7**

7. Use a rotary cutter to trim outer edges exactly on the outermost cutting lines of pattern with the paper side up.

8. Repeat steps 2–7 to complete two each E, F, G and H units; remove paper.

Completing the Top

1. Sew an H to each DR and a G to each D as shown in Figure 8; press seams toward G and H.

Figure 8

2. Turn the curved edge of the E and F pieces ¼" to the wrong side; baste to hold.

3. Pin and hand-stitch an E piece to each D, and an F piece to each DR as marked on pattern for positioning and referring to Figure 9 to complete D and DR units.

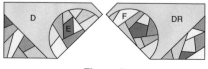

Figure 9

4. Sew a D unit to a DR unit, stopping stitching at the end of the marked seam line at the E and F ends as shown in Figure 10; press seam to one side. Repeat with second set of D and DR pieces.

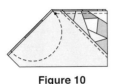

Figure 10

5. Set a fan unit into the pieced D/DR unit to complete half the runner center; press seams toward the fan units. Repeat to complete the second half of the runner center.

6. Join the two runner-center halves; press seam to one side.

7. To make one prairie point, fold each prairie-point square in half to make a rectangle; fold each corner to the center as shown in Figure 11. Press and baste to hold. Repeat to make 20 prairie points.

Figure 11

8. Position five prairie points each along one edge of L and LR pieces, spacing evenly between dots as marked on L and LR as shown in Figure 12; baste to hold in place.

Figure 12

9. Cut a piece of lace to fit each K and KR piece; baste in place on one edge of each K and KR piece as shown in Figure 13.

Figure 13

10. Sew K to L and KR to LR as shown in Figure 14; press seams toward K and KR.

Figure 14

11. Sew K-L and KR-LR pieces to the ends of the pieced center, mitering seams at the center as shown in Figure 15.

Figure 15

12. Center and sew M strips to opposite long sides of the pieced center; press seams toward M strips. Trim excess M to match L angles as shown in Figure 16.

Figure 16

13. Fold each length burgundy mottled spaghetti trim strips with right sides together along length and stitch a scant ¼" seam from the folded edge with a slightly shortened machine stitch. Trim excess seam allowance to ⅛"; turn right side out. Press flat.

14. Transfer spaghetti trim placement to the right side of N and NR; position and baste one 3" and three 4" lengths in place on each N and NR piece. Trim ends even with border strips.

15. Sew N and NR to corresponding L and LR edges, mitering seams at the center and taking care that spaghetti trim matches at the seam line.

16. Transfer outer edge scallop seam line to M and N borders; hand-baste just outside the marked scallop line.

Completing the Runner

1. Sandwich the batting between the completed top and prepared backing; pin or baste layers together.

2. Quilt as desired by hand or machine; remove pins or basting. Machine-baste exactly on the scallop seam line; trim all layers ¼" beyond stitching. Clip through layers to stitching at each inside corner.

3. Join bias binding strips on short ends to make one long strip; press seams open. Fold the strip in half along length with wrong sides together; press.

4. Sew binding to the right side of the runner edges, mitering corners and overlapping ends. Fold binding to the back side, stitching tassel cords securely into binding back-side seam allowance at each point and stitch in place to finish. ◈

L
Cut 4 cream mini-floral
(reverse 2 for LR)

Use this section for L

K
Cut 4 deep rose tonal
(reverse 2 for KR)

Use entire template
for K

Match to A seams at dots

C
Cut 2 pale pink stripe

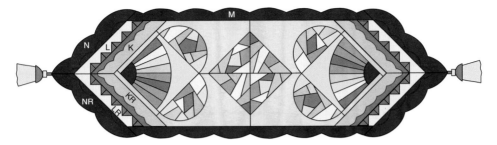

Vintage Hearts & Crazy Patches
Placement Diagram 42¼" x 14¼"

H Paper-Piecing Pattern
Make 3 copies

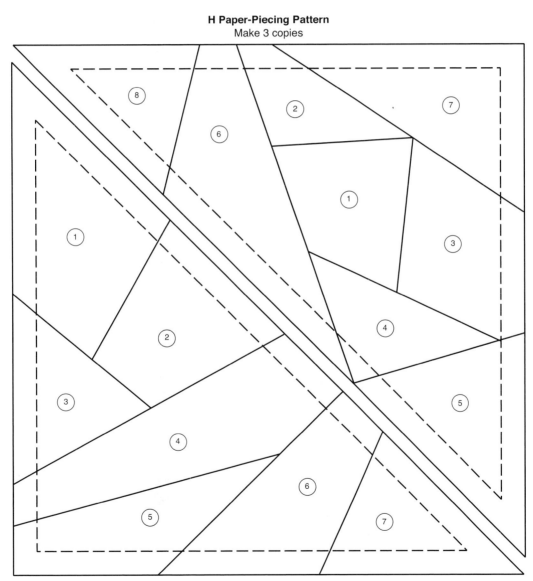

G Paper-Piecing Pattern
Make 3 copies

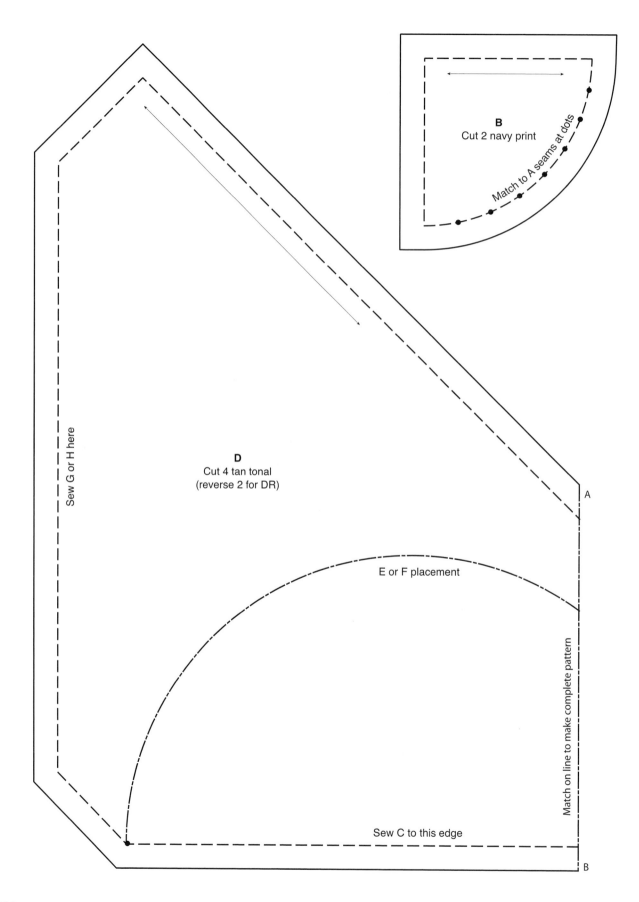

B
Cut 2 navy print

Match to A seams at dots

Sew G or H here

D
Cut 4 tan tonal
(reverse 2 for DR)

A

E or F placement

Match on line to make complete pattern

Sew C to this edge

B

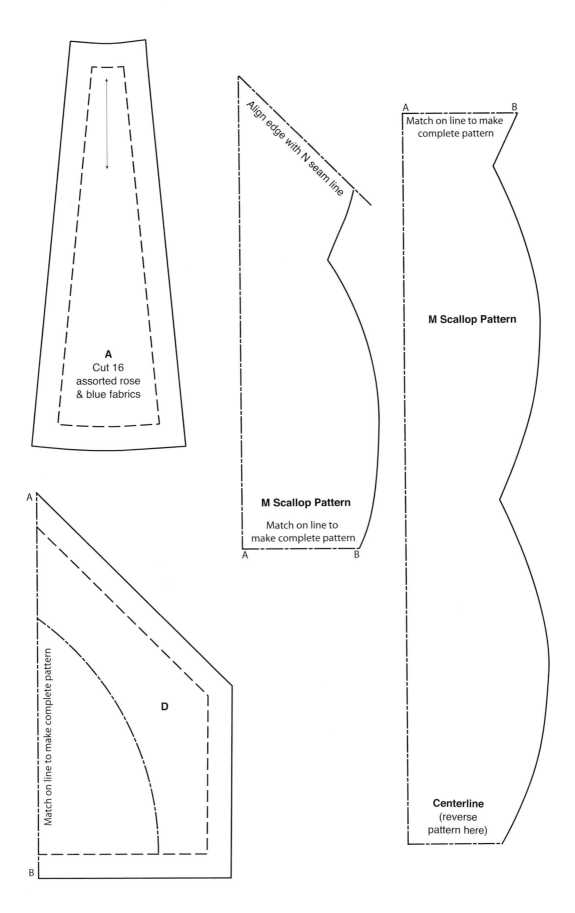

A
Cut 16
assorted rose
& blue fabrics

Align edge with N seam line

M Scallop Pattern

Match on line to
make complete pattern

A   B

M Scallop Pattern

Match on line to make
complete pattern

A   B

Match on line to make complete pattern

D

A

B

Centerline
(reverse
pattern here)

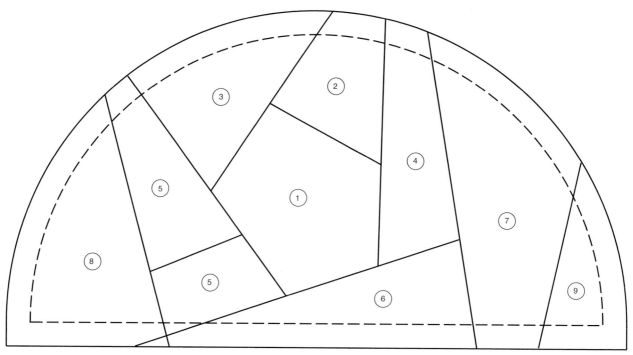

F Paper-Piecing Pattern
Make 3 copies

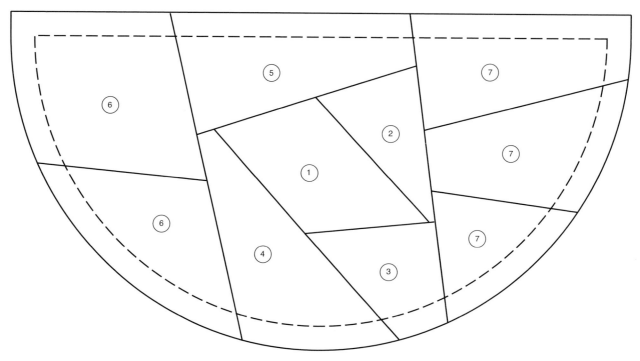

E Paper-Piecing Pattern
Make 3 copies

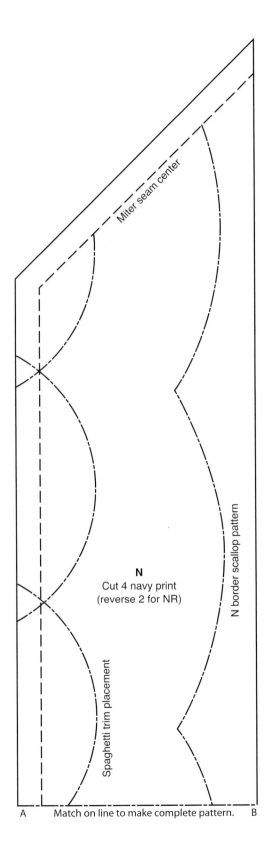

Miter seam center

N
Cut 4 navy print
(reverse 2 for NR)

N border scallop pattern

Spaghetti trim placement

A   Match on line to make complete pattern.   B

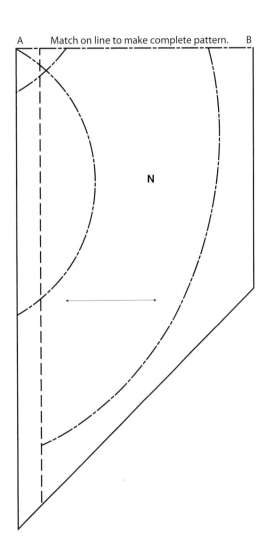

A   Match on line to make complete pattern.   B

N

Snow Crystals Table Runner

Design by Christine Schultz

Paper-pieced snowflakes in two sizes
are used in this pretty wintertime runner.

Project Specifications
Skill Level: Intermediate
Runner Size: 44" x 14½"

Materials
- ¾ yard white tonal
- 1½ yards blue batik
- Batting 50" x 21"
- Backing 50" x 21"
- All-purpose thread to match fabrics
- Quilting thread
- Basic sewing tools and supplies

Cutting
1. Prepare templates using patterns given; cut as directed on each piece.

2. See Completing the Paper-Piecing for cutting pieces for A, B and C units.

3. Cut three ¾" by fabric width strips white tonal; subcut strips into two each 34" K, 8" L and 6" M pieces.

4. Cut three 2½" by fabric width strips blue batik; subcut strips into two each 35" N, 10" O and 11" P strips.

5. Cut three 2¼" by fabric width strips blue batik for binding.

Completing the Paper-Piecing
1. Make copies of paper-piecing patterns as directed; cut one copy on marked lines to create templates for pieces.

2. Set stitch length to 18–20 stitches per inch; change needle to size 90—the larger needle will help perforate the paper and make paper removal easier.

3. Using the cut pieces as guides, cut pieces to fit in each numbered area of the A unit plus a ¼" seam allowance all around referring to pattern for color. Place the patterns with printed side up on the wrong side of fabric when cutting.

4. Lay piece 1 right side up over space 1 on the unprinted side of the paper pattern, with one longer raw edge of piece 1 extending beyond the seam line between pieces 1 and 2 as shown in Figure 1.

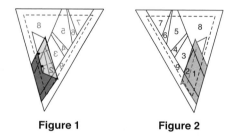

Figure 1   **Figure 2**

5. Pin piece 2 right sides together with piece 1 along the line between 1 and 2.

6. Flip pinned paper pattern over and sew on the line between spaces 1 and 2, extending stitches slightly beyond both ends as shown in Figure 2. Clip threads and press piece 2 to the right side; check to be sure spaces 1 and 2 are completely covered before adding piece 3.

7. Continue adding pieces in numerical order until the paper pattern is complete; press without steam. Use a rotary cutter to trim outer edges exactly on the outermost cutting lines of pattern with the paper side up.

8. Repeat steps 3–7 to complete 18 each A, B and C paper-pieced units.

Completing the Top

1. Sew an A unit to a B unit as shown in Figure 3; press seam in one direction. Repeat to make 18 A-B units.

Figure 3

2. Join three A-B units to make a large half-crystal unit as shown in Figure 4; press seams in one direction. Repeat to make six units.

Figure 4   **Figure 5**

3. Join three C units to make one small half-crystal unit as shown in Figure 5; press seams in one direction. Repeat to make six units.

4. Lay out large and small half-crystal units with pieces D–J and piece first in units and then in rows referring to Figure 6 for positioning and stitching; join the rows to complete the pieced center. Press seams away from the paper-pieced units wherever possible.

Figure 6

5. Carefully remove paper from pieced snowflakes.

Completing the Runner

1. Center and sew a K strip to opposite long sides of the pieced center; press seams toward K. Trim excess at each end continuing the angle of the end of the runner as shown in Figure 7.

Figure 7

2. Sew L and M strips to opposite short ends pressing seams toward strips after each addition and trimming excess as in step 1.

3. Center and sew an N strip to opposite long sides of the pieced center; press seams toward N. Trim excess as in step 1.

4. Add O and P strips to opposite short ends as in step 2 to complete the pieced top.

5. Sandwich the batting between the completed top and prepared backing; pin or baste layers together.

6. Quilt as desired by hand or machine; remove pins or basting. Trim excess backing and batting even with runner top.

7. Join binding strips on short ends to make one long strip; press seams open. Fold the strip in half along length with wrong sides together; press.

8. Sew binding to the right side of the runner edges, mitering corners and overlapping ends. Fold binding to the back side and stitch in place to finish. ◈

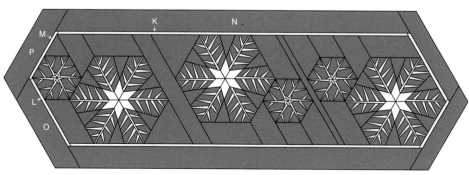

Snow Crystals Table Runner
Placement Diagram 44" x 14½"

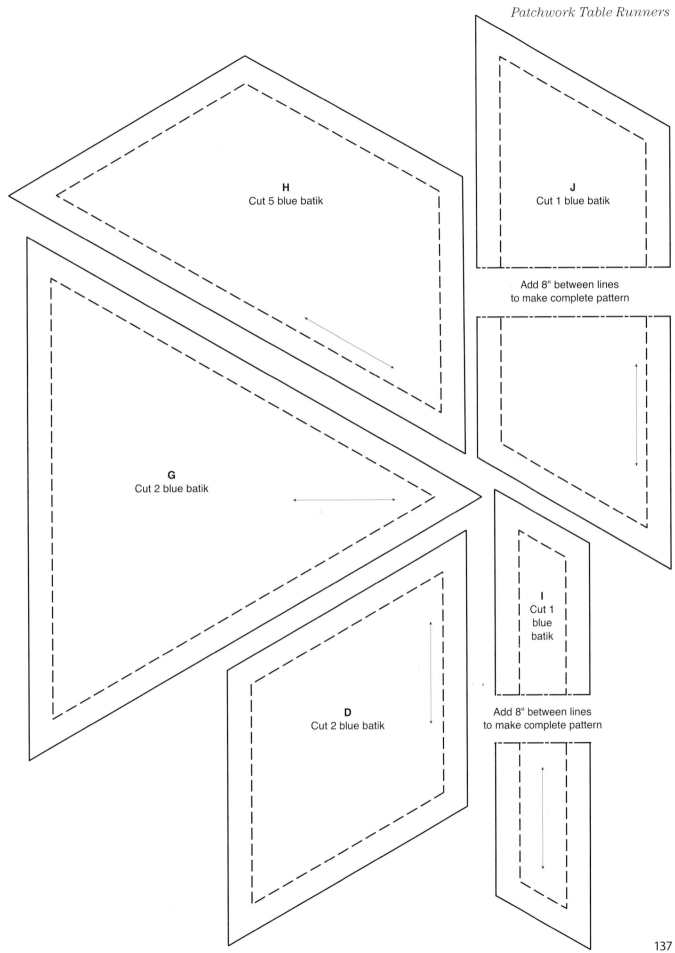

H
Cut 5 blue batik

J
Cut 1 blue batik

Add 8" between lines
to make complete pattern

G
Cut 2 blue batik

I
Cut 1
blue
batik

Add 8" between lines
to make complete pattern

D
Cut 2 blue batik

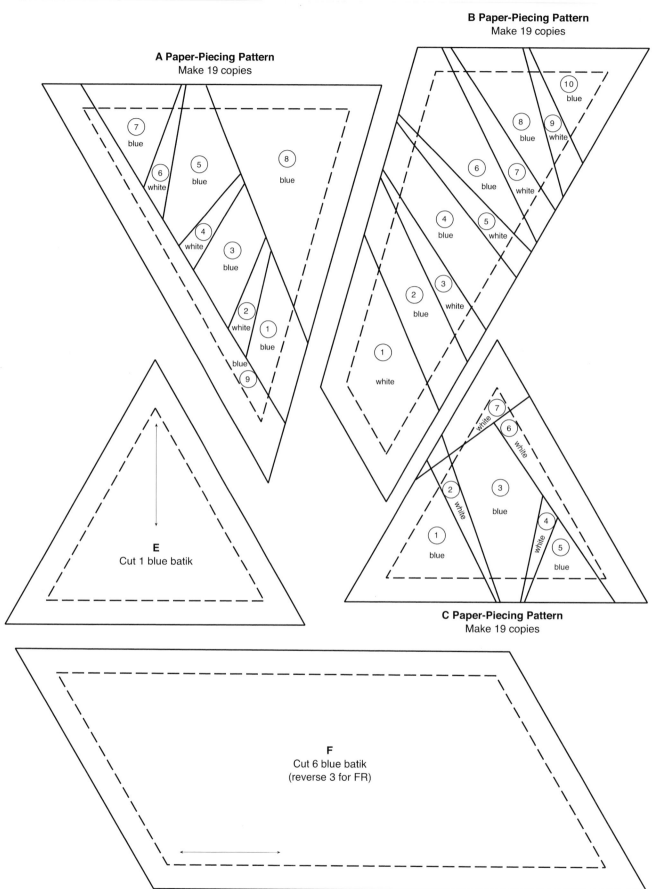

A Paper-Piecing Pattern
Make 19 copies

7
blue

5
blue

6
white

8
blue

4
white

3
blue

2
white

1
blue

blue

9

B Paper-Piecing Pattern
Make 19 copies

10
blue

8
blue

9
white

6
blue

7
white

4
blue

5
white

2
blue

3
white

1
white

7
white

6
white

white

2
white

3
blue

4
white

1
blue

5
blue

C Paper-Piecing Pattern
Make 19 copies

E
Cut 1 blue batik

F
Cut 6 blue batik
(reverse 3 for FR)

Through the Year

If you want to make your celebrations extra special, stitch a runner that fits the occasion: Christmas, Halloween, summer cookouts, autumn events. These runners make perfect gifts for friends and family.

Holiday Table Runner

Design by Connie Kauffman

A large open center and two smaller open squares give plenty of space to showcase a beautiful holiday print.

Project Specifications
Skill Level: Intermediate
Runner Size: 48" x 30"

Materials
- ¼ yard gold print
- ¼ yard red print
- ½ yard large holiday print
- ⅝ yard green print
- Batting 54" x 36"
- Backing 54" x 36"
- Neutral-color all-purpose thread
- Quilting thread
- Basic sewing tools and supplies

Cutting
1. Cut two 2⅜" by fabric width strips gold print; subcut strips into (22) 2⅜" squares. Cut each square in half on one diagonal to make 44 F triangles.

2. Cut two 2⅜" by fabric width strips red print; subcut strips into (20) 2⅜" squares. Cut each square in half on one diagonal to make 40 J triangles.

3. Cut nine 2" by fabric width strips green print; subcut strips into the following: eight 2" B squares and (10) 3½" C, four 5" D, (18) 6½" E, six 9½" H, four 11" I and two 12½" K rectangles.

4. Cut one 11⅛" by fabric width strip large holiday print; subcut strip into one 11⅛" A square and two 6⅞" x 6⅞" G squares.

Completing the Units
1. Join two J triangles as shown in Figure 1; press seam open. Repeat to make two J units.

Make 2

Figure 1

2. Sew a J triangle to the ends of two each C, E, H and K rectangles as shown in Figure 2; press seams open.

Make 2 each

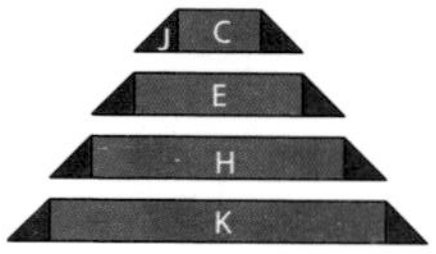

Figure 2

3. Join the units as shown in Figure 3 to complete two side units; press seams open. Set aside.

Side Unit
Make 2

Figure 3

4. Arrange and join E, H and I rectangles with F and J triangles as shown in Figure 4; press seams open.

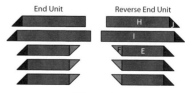

End Unit   Reverse End Unit

Figure 4

Tip

Make a gift for a friend in holiday or seasonal colors if you don't know the perfect colors to match their decor.

~Connie Kauffman

5. Join pieces to make two each end and reverse end units as shown in Figure 5; press seams open.

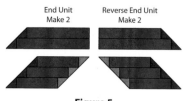

Figure 5

6. Arrange and join B squares and C, D and E rectangles with F triangles as shown in Figure 6 to make two each center and reverse center units; press seams open.

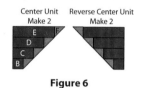

Figure 6

7. Arrange and join B squares and C rectangles with F triangles to make two each corner and reverse corner units as shown in Figure 7; press seams open.

Figure 7

Completing the Top

1. Arrange and sew the center and reverse center units to the A square as shown in Figure 8; press seams toward A.

Figure 8

2. Arrange and sew the corner and reverse corner units to G squares as shown in Figure 9; press seams toward G.

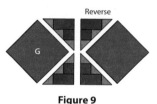

Figure 9

3. Arrange and sew the end and reverse end units to the remaining sides of the G squares, using a Y seam referring to Figure 10; press seams toward G. Attach H-I sections to top and bottom again referring to Figure 10.

Figure 10

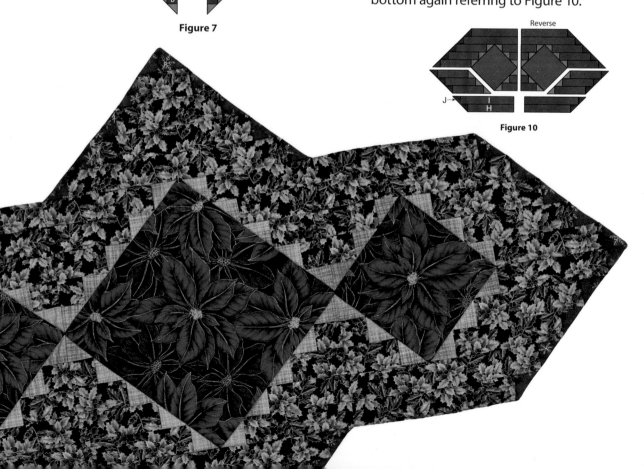

4. Sew the G units to the A unit as shown in Figure 11; press seams toward G units.

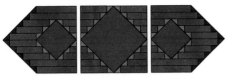

Figure 11

5. Sew the pieced side units to the sides of the A/G unit to complete the runner top referring to Figure 12; press seams toward the A/G unit.

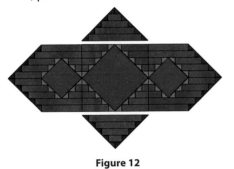

Figure 12

Completing the Runner

1. Layer batting, backing right side up and runner right side down; pin edges.

2. Sew all around, leaving a 4" opening along one side; trim batting and backing close to runner edges. Clip inner corners.

3. Turn right side out through opening; press edges flat.

4. Turn opening edges to the inside; hand-stitch closed.

5. Quilt as desired by hand or machine to finish. ◈

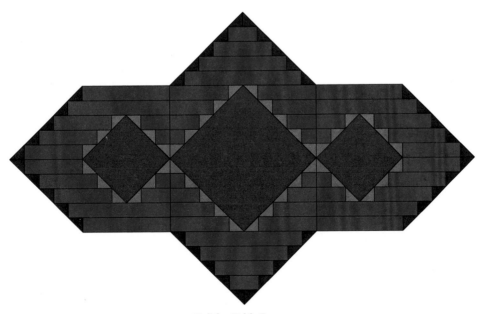

Holiday Table Runner
Placement Diagram 48" x 30"

Poinsettia & Holly Runner

Design by Barbara Clayton

Display a poinsettia plant in the center of this beautiful holiday runner.

Project Specifications
Skill Level: Intermediate
Runner Size: 31½" x 13⅞"
Block Size: 6¼" x 6¼"
Number of Blocks: 2

Materials
- Scraps red solid and gold print
- ⅛ yard green mottled
- ⅛ yard dark green mottled
- ⅛ yard red mottled
- ¼ yard red-with-white print
- ⅜ yard red-and-white stripe
- ½ yard white-with-red dots
- ⅝ yard red/burgundy mottled
- Batting 38" x 20"
- Backing 38" x 20"
- All-purpose thread to match fabrics
- Clear .004 invisible thread
- Quilting thread
- Freezer paper
- Water-soluble glue stick
- Water-erasable marker
- Sponge or cloth
- Basic sewing tools and supplies and water-erasable marker

Cutting
1. Cut two 6¾" x 6¾" A squares white-with-red dot.

2. Cut two 2" by fabric width strips each white-with-red dot (G) and red-with-white print (H). Cut two 2" x 2" I squares from each G strip and two 2" x 2⅜" J pieces from each H strip.

3. Cut four identical 3⅝" x 3⅝" B squares red-and-white stripe with stripes on the diagonal of the squares as shown in Figure 1.

Figure 1

4. Cut two 1½" x 27" E strips and two 1½" x 11⅜" F strips red-and-white stripe.

5. Cut one 10⅛" x 10⅛" square red/burgundy mottled; cut the square in half on both diagonals to make four C triangles.

6. Cut two 5⅜" x 5⅜" squares red/burgundy mottled; cut each square in half on one diagonal to make four D triangles.

7. Cut three 2¼" by fabric width strips red/burgundy mottled for binding.

Completing the Appliqué
1. Trace the petal, leaf, center, holly leaf and berry shapes onto the paper side of the freezer paper; layer paper and cut several layers at a time to cut the number of pieces needed for each shape as directed on patterns.

2. Press the waxy side of the freezer-paper shapes onto the wrong side of fabrics as directed on patterns.

3. Cut out shapes, adding ¼" all around freezer-paper patterns when cutting; clip curves, points and indentations almost to the paper patterns.

4. Using the water-soluble glue stick, glue the ¼" excess fabric over the edge and to the back of the freezer paper, gluing all the way around each shape. Set aside the holly leaves and berries.

5. Fold and crease each A square to mark the center. Using the Poinsettia Motif pattern as a guide, center and pin the poinsettia petals, leaves and center on one A square. Repeat with second motif on the second A square.

6. Using clear invisible thread, stitch around the outside edge of each appliqué shape with a narrow blind hemstitch.

7. Turn the A squares to the back side and make a slit behind each shape; trim away backing fabric to ¼" from the edge of the stitching around the shapes.

8. Use a sponge or cloth to wet the back of each shape; tear away the freezer paper. Let dry and steam or lightly press on a folded towel.

Completing the Top

1. Join two B squares as shown in Figure 2; press seam in one direction. Repeat. Join the two units to complete the B unit, again referring to Figure 2.

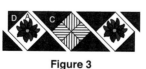

Figure 2   Figure 3

2. Arrange and join the appliquéd A squares and B unit with the C and D triangles in diagonal rows as shown in Figure 3; press seams away from A and B. Join the rows to complete the pieced center; press seams toward the B row.

3. Sew an E strip to opposite long sides and F strips to opposite short ends; press seams toward E and F strips.

4. Sew a G strip to an H strip with right sides together along length; press seams toward H strip. Repeat to make two strip sets.

5. Subcut the G-H strip sets into (26) 2" G-H units as shown in Figure 4.

Figure 4

6. Join nine G-H units to make a side strip; press seams in one direction. Add an I square to one end of the strip as shown in Figure 5. Repeat to make two side strips.

Figure 5

7. Sew a side strip to opposite long sides of the pieced center referring to the Placement Diagram for positioning of strips; press seams toward E strips.

8. Join four G-H units and a J piece to make an end strip as shown in Figure 6; press seams in one direction. Repeat to make two end strips.

Figure 6

9. Sew an end strip to opposite short ends of the pieced center to complete the pieced top, referring to the Placement Diagram for positioning of strips; press seams toward F strips.

10. Arrange and pin three berries and two holly leaves in a cluster on each C and D triangle, extending leaves into the E and F borders referring to the Placement Diagram for positioning.

11. Appliqué in place and remove freezer paper as in steps 6–8 for Completing the Appliqué to complete the pieced top.

Completing the Runner

1. Sandwich the batting between the completed top and prepared backing; pin or baste layers together to hold.

2. Quilt as desired by hand or machine; remove pins or basting. Trim excess backing and batting even with runner top. **Note:** *The sample runner was hand-quilted using red and white quilting thread. Appliqué shapes were outline-quilted ¼" away from edge of shapes.*

3. Join binding strips on short ends to make one long strip; press seams open. Fold the strip in half along length with wrong sides together; press.

4. Sew binding to runner edges, overlapping ends. Fold binding to the back side and hand-stitch in place to finish. ◈

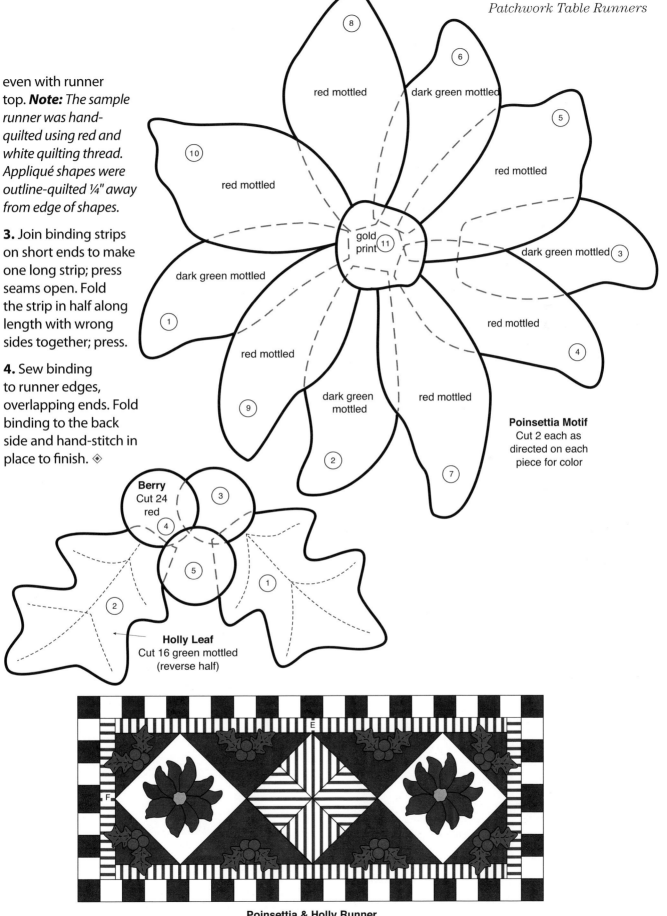

Poinsettia Motif
Cut 2 each as directed on each piece for color

Berry
Cut 24
red

Holly Leaf
Cut 16 green mottled
(reverse half)

Poinsettia & Holly Runner
Placement Diagram 31½" x 13⅞"

Heartfelt Table Runner

Design by Connie Kauffman

Pieced heart blocks interlock with the center unit to make this unusual runner.

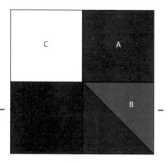

Heart
6" x 6" Block
Make 6

Project Specifications
Skill Level: Beginner
Runner Size: 40⅜" x 23⅜"
Block Size: 6" x 6"
Number of Blocks: 6

Materials
- 1 (3" x 3") red-scrap E square
- 6 (3⅞" x 3⅞") red-scrap B squares
- 12 (3½" x 3½") red-scrap A squares
- ⅛ yard red-with-white dot
- ⅜ yard white-with-red blotches
- Batting 42" x 25"
- Backing 42" x 25"
- All-purpose thread to match fabric
- Quilting thread
- 2 (1") heart buttons
- Basic sewing tools and supplies

Cutting
1. Cut each B square in half on one diagonal to make 12 B triangles.

2. Cut one 3½" by fabric width strip white-with-red blotches; subcut strip into six 3½" C squares.

3. Cut one 3" by fabric width strip white-with-red blotches; subcut strip into four 6½" D rectangles.

4. Cut two 1½" by fabric width strips white-with-red blotches; subcut strip into two 8½" J strips, two 5½" I strips and four 6½" H strips.

5. Cut two 1½" by fabric width strips red-with-white dot; subcut strips into two 15" F strips and two 16" G strips.

Completing the Blocks
1. Select two different B triangles; join along the diagonal to make a B unit as shown in Figure 1; press seam in one direction.

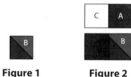

Figure 1   **Figure 2**

2. Select two different A squares; sew one to C and one to the B unit as shown in Figure 2; press seam toward A in each unit.

3. Join the two pieced units to complete one Heart block referring to the block drawing; press seam toward the A-C unit.

4. Repeat steps 1–3 to complete six Heart blocks.

Completing the Top
1. Join two Heart blocks with D to make a block row as shown in Figure 3; press seams away from D. Repeat to make two block rows.

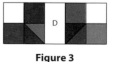

Figure 3

2. Sew E between two D rectangles to make a D-E row; press seams toward E.

Tip

Use a seasonal fabric for the backing to make a reversible runner.

~Connie Kauffman

3. Sew the D-E row between the block rows to complete the center unit referring to the Placement Diagram for positioning of rows; press seams toward the D-E row.

4. Sew the F, G, H, I and J strips to the center unit and the remaining blocks as shown in Figure 4; press seams toward strips.

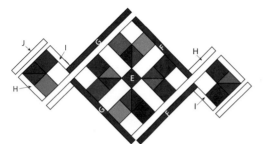

Figure 4

5. Sew the side blocks to the center unit to complete the pieced top referring to the Placement Diagram for positioning; press seams away from the center unit.

Completing the Runner

1. Place backing piece right side up on batting; place completed top right sides together with backing; pin edges.

2. Trim backing and batting even with the pieced top.

3. Sew all around, leaving a 4" opening along one side; clip inner corners. Trim batting close to stitching.

4. Turn right side out through opening; press edges flat.

5. Turn opening edges to the inside; hand-stitch opening closed.

6. Quilt as desired by hand or machine. ***Note:*** *A continuous-line heart-quilting pattern is given. It was machine-quilted into the A-B area of each block.*

7. Sew a heart button to the side-block C squares to finish. ◈

Continuous-Line Heart Quilting Pattern

Heartfelt Table Runner
Placement Diagram 40³/₈" x 23³/₈"

Stars in My Heart

Design by Julie Weaver

Add a little patriotic spirit to your table setting for your Fourth of July celebration.

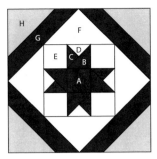

Star
9" x 9" Block
Make 2

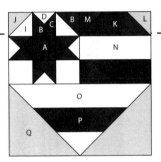

Heart
9" x 9" Block
Make 2

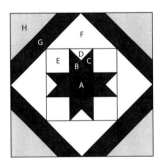

Reverse Star
9" x 9" Block
Make 1

Project Specifications
Skill Level: Intermediate
Runner Size: 53" x 17"
Block Size: 9" x 9"
Number of Blocks: 5

Materials
- ⅓ yard blue stripe
- ⅓ yard red print
- ⅜ yard tan print
- ½ yard cream tonal
- 1 yard blue print
- Batting 59" x 23"
- Backing 59" x 23"
- Neutral-color all-purpose thread
- Quilting thread
- Basic sewing tools and supplies

Cutting
1. Cut one 2¾" by fabric width strips red print; subcut strip into six 2¾" C squares, four 2½" x 2½" W squares and five 2" x 2" A squares.

2. Cut one 2" by fabric width strip red print; subcut strip into four 5" K pieces and two 9½" P pieces.

3. Cut one 1½" by fabric width strip red print; subcut strip into eight 1½" T squares.

4. Cut one 2⅜" by fabric width strip blue print; subcut strip into (13) 2⅜" B squares and two 2" x 2" M squares.

5. Cut one 5⅜" by fabric width strip blue print; subcut strip into six 5⅜" G squares.

6. Cut five 1½" by fabric width R/X strips blue print.

7. Cut two 1½" by fabric width strips blue print; subcut strips into two 9½" S strips and two 15½" Y strips.

8. Cut four 2¼" by fabric width strips blue print for binding.

9. Cut one 2¾" by fabric width strip cream tonal; subcut strip into six 2¾" D squares and two 2⅜" I squares.

10. Cut two 2" by fabric width strips cream tonal; subcut strips into (16) 2" E squares, two 5" N pieces and four 9½" O pieces.

11. Cut one 4⅛" by fabric width strip cream tonal; subcut strip into six 4⅛" squares. Cut each square in half on one diagonal to make 12 F triangles.

12. Cut one 3½" by fabric width strip tan print; subcut strip into (12) 3½" H squares.

13. Cut one 5" by fabric width strip tan print; subcut strip into four 5" Q squares, one 2⅜" x 2⅜" J square and two 2" x 2" L squares.

14. Cut three 2½" by fabric width U/V strips blue stripe; subcut two 11½" V strips from one strip.

Completing the Star Blocks

1. Draw a diagonal line from corner to corner on the back side of each D square.

2. Place a D square right sides together with a C square and stitch ¼" on each side of the marked line as shown in Figure 1; repeat for all C and D squares.

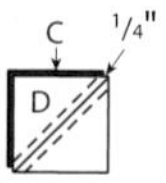

Figure 1

3. Cut apart on the marked line to make 12 C-D units as shown in Figure 2; open and press with seam toward C.

Figure 2

4. Draw a diagonal line across the seam on the back side of the C-D units as shown in Figure 3.

Figure 3

5. Place a marked C-D unit right sides together with a B square and sew ¼" on each side of the marked line as shown in Figure 4; cut apart on the marked line, open and press to make one each B-C-D and reverse B-C-D unit, again referring to Figure 4. Repeat with remaining C-D units and B squares to make 12 each B-C-D and reverse B-C-D units; set aside four B-C-D units for another project.

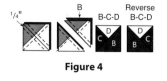

Figure 4

6. Draw a diagonal line from corner to corner on the wrong side of each H square.

7. Place an H square right sides together on opposite corners of G as shown in Figure 5, stitch on the marked line. Trim seam to ¼" and press H to the right side.

8. Mark a diagonal line from corner to corner through the center of the G-H unit; cut on the marked line to make two G-H units, again referring to Figure 5. Repeat steps 7 and 8 to complete 12 G-H units.

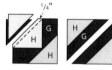

Figure 5

9. To complete one Star block, join two B-C-D units with A to make the center row as shown in Figure 6; press seams toward A.

Figure 6

10. Sew E to opposite sides of a B-C-D unit to make the top row as shown in Figure 7; press seams toward E. Repeat to make the bottom row.

Figure 7

11. Sew the center row between the top and bottom rows to complete one star unit referring to Figure 8; press seams away from the center row.

Figure 8

12. Sew F to each side of the star unit; press seams toward F.

13. Sew a G-H unit to each side of the star unit to complete one Star block referring to the block drawing; press seams toward G-H units.

14. Repeat steps 9–13 to complete a second star block.

15. Repeat steps 9–13 to complete one Reverse Star block using reverse B-C-D units referring to Figure 9 for placement of units when joining.

Figure 9

16. Set aside remaining reverse B-C-D units for Heart blocks.

Completing the Heart Blocks

1. Mark a diagonal line from corner to corner on the wrong side of each I square.

2. Referring to Figure 10, place an I square right sides together with a J square; stitch ¼" on each side of the marked line. Cut apart on the marked line to make two I-J units.

Figure 10

3. Repeat step 2 to make two B-I units, again referring to Figure 10.

4. To complete one Heart block, sew an A square between two reverse B-C-D units to make a center row as shown in Figure 11; press seam toward A.

Figure 11

5. Sew a reverse B-C-D unit between two E squares to make the bottom row as shown in Figure 12; press seams toward E.

Figure 12   **Figure 13**

6. Sew a reverse B-C-D unit between an I-J and B-I unit to make the top row as shown in Figure 13; press seams toward I-J and B-I units.

7. Sew the center row between the top and bottom rows to complete one star unit as shown in Figure 14; press seams in one direction.

Figure 14

8. Sew N between two K pieces to make a K-N unit as shown in Figure 15; press seams toward K.

Figure 15

9. Mark a diagonal line from corner to corner on the wrong side of each L and M square.

10. Place L and M squares right sides together on the K-N unit and stitch on the marked line as shown in Figure 16; trim seam to ¼" and press L and M to the right side to complete the K-N-L-M unit.

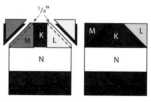

Figure 16

11. Sew P between two O strips; press seams toward P.

12. Mark a diagonal line from corner to corner on the wrong side of each Q square.

13. Referring to Figure 17, place a Q square on one corner of the O-P unit; stitch on the marked line. Trim seam to ¼" and press Q to the right side. Repeat on the remaining end to complete an O-P-Q unit.

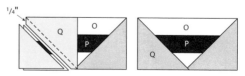

Figure 17

14. Sew the star unit to the K-N-L-M unit and add the O-P-Q unit to complete one Heart block as shown in Figure 18; press seams away from the star unit.

Figure 18

15. Repeat steps 4–14 to complete two Heart blocks.

Completing the Top

1. Sew a Star block to opposite sides of the Reverse Star block; add a Heart block to each end to complete the pieced center referring to the Placement Diagram for positioning of blocks; press seams in one direction.

2. Join the R/X strips with right sides together on short ends to make one long strip; press seams open. Subcut strip into two 45½" R strips and two 51½" X strips.

3. Sew an R strip to opposite long sides of the pieced center; press seams toward R strips.

4. Sew a T square to each end of each S strip and each Y strip; press seams toward S and Y.

5. Sew an S-T strip to opposite short ends of the pieced center; press seams toward S-T strips.

6. Join the U strips with right sides together on short ends to make one long strip; press seams open. Subcut strips into two 47½" U strips.

7. Sew the U strips to opposite long sides of the pieced center; press seams toward U strips.

8. Sew a W square to each end of each V strip; press seams toward V strips.

9. Sew a V-W strip to opposite short ends of the pieced center; press seams toward V-W strips.

10. Sew X strips to opposite long sides and T-Y strips to opposite short ends of the pieced center to complete the pieced top; press seams toward X and T-Y strips.

Completing the Runner

1. Sandwich the batting between the completed top and prepared backing; pin or baste layers together.

2. Quilt as desired by hand or machine; remove pins or basting. Trim excess backing and batting even with runner top.

3. Join binding strips on short ends to make one long strip; press seams open. Fold the strip in half along length with wrong sides together; press.

4. Sew binding to the right side of the runner edges, mitering corners and overlapping ends. Fold binding to the back side and stitch in place. ◈

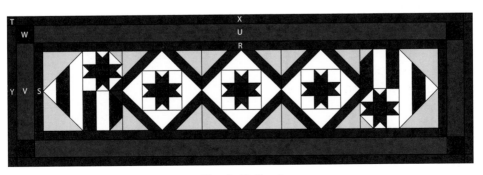

Stars in My Heart
Placement Diagram 53" x 17"

Cookout Table Runner

Design by Jennifer Foltz

Make the perfect table runner for your next backyard cookout.

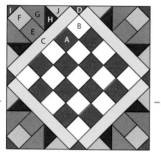

Picnic
16" x 16" Block
Make 1

Project Specifications
Skill Level: Intermediate
Runner Size: 46" x 18"
Block Size: 16" x 16"
Number of Blocks: 1

Materials
- Scrap black solid
- ⅛ yard each orange and dark brown tonals
- ¼ yard each tan, white, and light and dark green tonals
- ⅜ yard purple mottled
- ½ yard yellow tonal
- ⅞ yard red tonal
- Batting 52" x 24"
- Backing 52" x 24"
- Neutral-color and black all-purpose thread
- Quilting thread
- Brown embroidery floss
- 8" square fusible web
- 10" square fabric stabilizer
- 24 black shiny teardrop beads
- Basic sewing tools and supplies

Cutting
1. Cut one 2½" by fabric width strip red tonal; subcut strip into (12) 2½" A squares.

2. Cut one 3" by fabric width strip red tonal; subcut strip into one 3" D square and (32) 1½" x 1½" O squares. Cut the D square on both diagonals to make four D triangles.

3. Cut one 3½" by fabric width strip red tonal; subcut strip into eight 3½" P squares and two 2⅜" x 2⅜" I squares. Cut each I square in half on one diagonal to make four I triangles.

4. Cut three 1½" by fabric width W/X strips red tonal.

5. Cut four 2¼" by fabric width strips red tonal for binding.

6. Cut one 2½" by fabric width strip white tonal; subcut strip into (13) 2½" B squares.

7. Cut one 1¾" by fabric width strip white tonal; subcut strip into two 21" S strips.

8. Cut one 1¾" by fabric width strip yellow tonal; subcut strip into four 10½" C strips.

9. Cut three 3" by fabric width strips yellow tonal; subcut strips into (16) 5½" R rectangles and four 1½" x 1½" Y squares.

10. Cut one 1¼" by fabric width L strip yellow tonal.

11. Cut one 2½" by fabric width strip orange tonal; subcut strip into four 2½" E squares.

12. Cut one 4⅛" by fabric width strip light green tonal; subcut strip into two 4⅛" J squares and four 2½" x 2½" F squares. Cut each J square on both diagonals to make eight J triangles.

13. Cut one 1¼" by fabric width M strip light green tonal.

14. Cut one 4½" by fabric width strip dark green tonal; subcut strip into eight 2" Q rectangles and four 3¾" x 3¾" G squares. Cut each G square in half on one diagonal to make eight G triangles.

15. Cut one 4⅛" by fabric width strip purple mottled; subcut strip into two 4⅛" squares. Cut each square on both diagonals to make eight H triangles.

16. Cut three 1½" by fabric width strips purple tonal; subcut strips into six 16½" V strips.

17. Cut one 2" by fabric width K strip dark brown tonal.

18. Cut one 1" by fabric width strip dark brown tonal; subcut one 21" T strip.

19. Cut two 1¾" by fabric width N strips tan tonal.

20. Cut one 2½" by fabric width strip tan tonal; subcut strip into eight 3½" U pieces.

21. Trace ant shapes onto the paper side of the fusible web; cut out shapes, leaving a margin around each one.

22. Fuse shapes to the scrap black solid; cut out shapes on traced lines. Remove paper backing.

Completing the Picnic Block

1. Join three A squares and two B squares to make an A row as shown in Figure 1; press seams toward A. Repeat to make two A rows.

Make 2

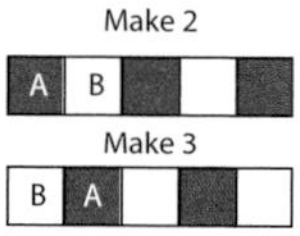

Make 3

Figure 1

2. Join three B squares and two A squares to make a B row, again referring to Figure 1; press seams toward A. Repeat to make three B rows.

3. Join the A and B rows as shown in Figure 2 to complete one A-B unit; press seams in one direction.

Figure 2

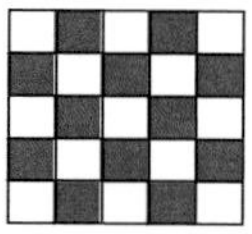

4. Sew a C strip to opposite sides of the A-B unit; press seams toward C strips.

5. Sew a D triangle to each end of the remaining C strips as shown in Figure 3; press seams toward C.

Figure 3

6. Sew a C-D strip to the remaining sides of the A-B unit to complete the block center; press seams toward the strips.

7. Sew E to F and add I to complete an E-F-I unit as shown in Figure 4; press seams away from I. Repeat to make four units.

Figure 4

8. Sew H to G and add J to complete an H-G-J unit as shown in Figure 5; repeat to make a reverse unit, again referring to Figure 5. Repeat to make four each H-G-J and reverse H-G-J units.

Make 4   Reverse Make 4

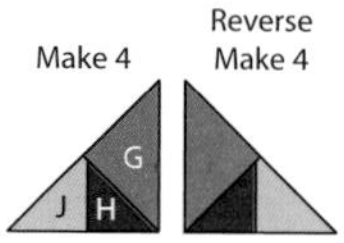

Figure 5

9. Sew an H-G-J unit and a reverse H-G-J unit to an E-F-I unit as shown in Figure 6 to complete one corner unit; press seams toward the H-G-J units. Repeat to make four corner units.

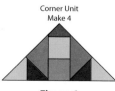
Corner Unit
Make 4

Figure 6

10. Sew a corner unit to each side of the block center to complete the Picnic block as shown in Figure 7; press seams away from the block center.

Figure 7

Completing the S'mores Strips

1. Sew the T strip between two S strips with right sides together along length; press seams toward T.

2. Subcut the S-T strip set into eight 2½" S-T units as shown in Figure 8.

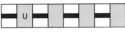

Figure 8

3. Join four S-T units with four U pieces as shown in Figure 9 to complete one s'mores strip; press seams toward U. Repeat to make two s'mores strips.

Figure 9

Completing the Watermelon Strips

1. Make eight copies of the watermelon paper-piecing pattern given.

2. Place P right side up on the unmarked side of one paper-piecing pattern; pin Q right sides together with P as shown in Figure 10.

Figure 10

3. Turn the paper over and stitch on the line between pieces P and Q as shown in Figure 11.

Figure 11

4. Turn paper over, trim seam to ¼" and press Q to the right side as shown in Figure 12.

Figure 12

5. Place an R rectangle right sides down on the fabric side of the stitched unit with edge of R extending ¼" beyond the stitching line between P/Q and R; pin along line and turn paper over to check placement before stitching. When satisfied with the placement of R, stitch on the line between pieces P/Q and R. Trim seam allowance to ¼" and press R to the right side.

6. Repeat step 5 with a second R on the opposite side of the unit.

7. Trim excess fabric and paper even with solid outer line on the paper pattern to complete one watermelon unit as shown in Figure 13.

Figure 13

8. Repeat steps 2–7 to complete eight watermelon units.

9. Join four watermelon units as shown in Figure 14 to make a watermelon strip; press seams in one direction. Repeat to make two watermelon strips.

Figure 14

Completing the Hamburger Strips

1. Fold and press each L and M strip with wrong sides together along length to make a double-layered strip.

2. Sew the folded L strip to one long side of K and the folded M strip to the opposite long side of the K strip with raw edges aligned and folded edges toward center of K.

3. Sew an N strip to opposite sides of the stitched strip set to complete a K-L-M-N strip set; press seams toward N.

4. Subcut the K-L-M-N strip set into eight 4½" K-L-M-N units as shown in Figure 15.

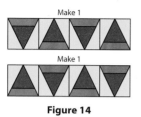

Figure 15

5. Draw a diagonal line from corner to corner on the wrong side of each O square.

6. Place an O square right sides together on each corner of a K-L-M-N unit and stitch on the marked line as shown in Figure 16; trim seam to ¼" and press O to the right side to complete a hamburger unit, again referring to Figure 16. Repeat to make eight hamburger units.

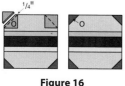

Figure 16

7. Join four hamburger units to make a hamburger strip as shown in Figure 17; press seams in one direction. Repeat to make two hamburger strips.

Figure 17

Completing the Top

1. Join the Picnic block with six V strips and the hamburger, watermelon and s'mores strips to complete the pieced center referring to the Placement Diagram for positioning of strips; press seams toward V strips.

2. Join the W/X strip with right sides together on short ends to make one long strip; press seams open. Subcut strip into two 18½" X strips and two 44½" W strips.

3. Sew a W strip to opposite long sides of the pieced center; press seams toward W strips.

4. Sew a Y square to each end of each X strip; press seams toward X strips.

5. Sew an X-Y strip to opposite short ends of the pieced top.

6. Arrange and fuse the three ant shapes on the Picnic block; pin the square of fabric stabilizer behind the shapes.

7. Using black thread and a machine buttonhole stitch, stitch ant shapes in place.

8. Using pattern as a guide, add legs to ants using a decorative machine stitch; remove fabric stabilizer.

9. Remove paper patterns from watermelon units.

Completing the Runner

1. Sandwich the batting between the completed top and prepared backing; pin or baste layers together.

2. Quilt as desired by hand or machine; remove pins or basting. Trim excess backing and batting even with runner top.

3. Join binding strips on short ends to make one long strip; press seams open. Fold the strip in half along length with wrong sides together; press.

4. Sew binding to the right side of the runner edges, mitering corners and overlapping ends. Fold binding to the back side and stitch in place.

5. Sew three teardrop beads to each watermelon unit.

6. Using 3 strands brown embroidery floss, make eight French knots on each s'more U rectangle, placing each one ½" from side edge and ⅜" apart to resemble graham crackers to finish. ◈

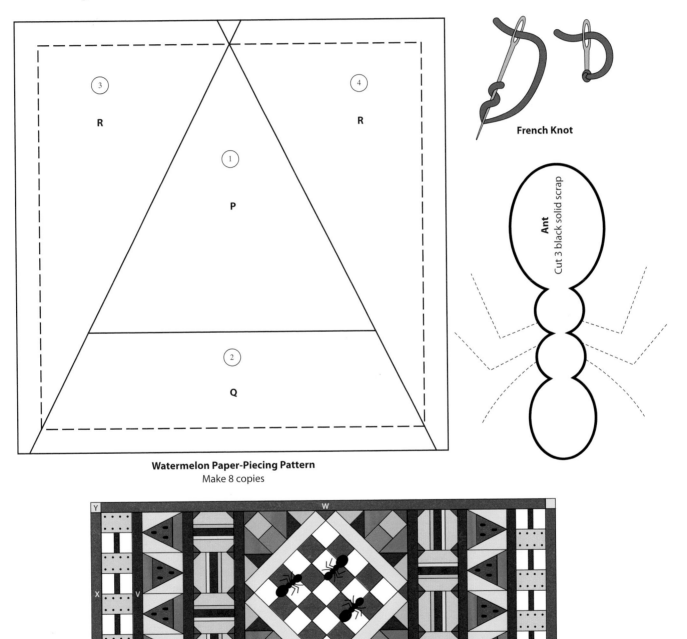

Watermelon Paper-Piecing Pattern
Make 8 copies

French Knot

Ant
Cut 3 black solid scrap

Cookout Table Runner
Placement Diagram 46" x 18"

Pumpkin
5½" x 5½" Block
Make 3

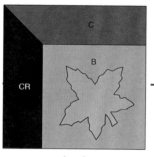

Leaf
5½" x 5½" Block
Make 10

Project Specifications
Skill Level: Beginner
Runner Size: 38¾" x 15½"
Block Size: 5½" x 5½"
Number of Blocks: 3 and 10

Materials
- Scraps bright orange, dark orange, rust, green and gold prints
- ¼ yard cream tonal
- ¼ yard tan/cream print
- ¼ yard light tan print
- ¼ yard dark tan print
- ⅓ yard dark brown/black print
- ⅓ yard chocolate brown print
- Batting 45" x 22"
- Backing 45" x 22"
- All-purpose thread to match fabrics
- Clear .004 nylon thread
- Quilting thread
- ½ yard 12"-wide fusible web
- ½ yard fabric stabilizer
- Water-erasable marker or pencil
- Basic sewing tools and supplies

Autumn Leaves & Pumpkins

Design by Barbara Clayton

Small appliquéd pumpkins and leaves create the design of this autumn runner.

Cutting
1. Cut three 6" A squares cream tonal.

2. Cut 4½" x 4½" B squares as follows: two tan/cream print, four light tan print and four dark tan print.

3. Prepare template for C/CR using pattern given; cut as directed, marking the dot from pattern onto each piece using the water-erasable marker or pencil.

Completing the Leaf Blocks
1. Sew a C and CR piece to two adjacent sides of each B square, starting at the square edge and stopping stitching with needle down at the dot as shown in Figure 1; pivot and stitch C/CR ends, again referring to Figure 1. Press seams toward B.

Figure 1

2. Trace leaf shapes onto the paper side of the fusible web referring to patterns for number to cut; cut out shapes, leaving a margin around each one. Fuse shapes to the wrong side of scraps as directed; cut out shapes on traced lines. Remove paper backing.

3. Arrange and fuse one leaf shape to each B-C-CR square referring to the Placement Diagram for positioning.

4. Cut (10) 4" x 4" squares fabric stabilizer; pin a square to the wrong side of each fused square.

5. Using a close satin stitch and thread to match leaf shapes, machine-stitch around each leaf shape to complete the 10 Leaf blocks.

Completing the Pumpkin Blocks

1. Prepare pumpkin appliqué shapes as for leaf shapes.

2. Referring to the pattern and block drawing, arrange and fuse shapes to the A squares in numerical order.

3. Cut four 5" x 5" squares fabric stabilizer; pin a square to the wrong side of each fused A square.

4. Machine-stitch pumpkin appliqué pieces in place as in step 5 for Completing the Leaf Blocks to complete three Pumpkin blocks.

Completing the Top

1. Arrange and join the completed blocks in rows as shown in Figure 2; press seams in adjacent rows in opposite directions.

2. Join the rows as stitched to complete the pieced top; press seams in one direction.

Completing the Runner

1. Place backing piece right side up on batting; place completed top right sides together with backing; pin edges.

2. Trim backing and batting even with the pieced top.

3. Sew all around, leaving a 4" opening along one side; clip inner corners. Trim batting close to stitching.

4. Turn right side out through opening; press edges flat.

5. Turn opening edges to the inside; hand-stitch opening closed.

6. Quilt as desired by hand or machine to finish. ❖

Figure 2

Leaf
Cut 4 gold

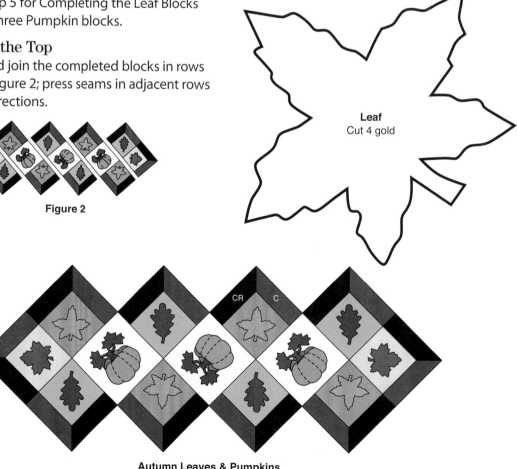

Autumn Leaves & Pumpkins
Placement Diagram 38³/₄" x 15¹/₂"

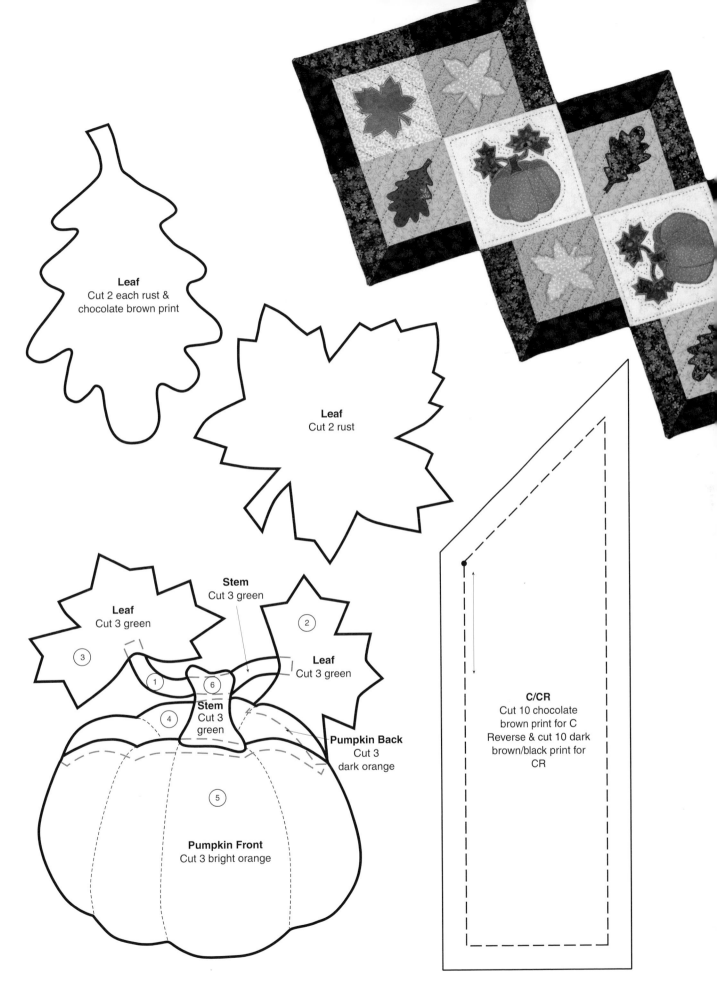

Leaf
Cut 2 each rust &
chocolate brown print

Leaf
Cut 2 rust

Leaf
Cut 3 green

③

Stem
Cut 3 green

Leaf
Cut 3 green

②

① ⑥

Stem
Cut 3
green

④

Pumpkin Back
Cut 3
dark orange

⑤

Pumpkin Front
Cut 3 bright orange

C/CR
Cut 10 chocolate
brown print for C
Reverse & cut 10 dark
brown/black print for
CR

Trick or Treat Runner

Design by Connie Kauffman

Make a reversible runner for Halloween this year.

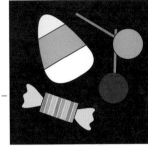

Halloween
9½" x 9½" Block
Make 2

Project Specifications
Skill Level: Beginner
Runner Size: 50" x 13½"
Block Size: 9½" x 9½"
Number of Blocks: 2

Materials
• Scraps green, white, orange, yellow, purple prints; coordinating stripe and tan solid
• 1 Jelly Roll Halloween-theme fabrics
• ⅜ yard black/orange print
• ½ yard black Halloween print
• Batting 56" x 20"
• All-purpose thread to match fabrics
• Quilting thread
• ½ yard fusible web
• ⅔ yard fabric stabilizer
• Basic sewing tools and supplies

Cutting
1. Cut one 10" by fabric width strip black/orange print; subcut strip into two 10" A squares and eight 2½" x 2½" C squares.

2. Cut one 14¾" x 14¾" square black Halloween print; cut the square in half on both diagonals to make four D triangles. Set aside two triangles for another project.

3. Cut (16) 13" B strips from the Jelly Roll strips. **Note:** *A Jelly Roll is made up of (40) 2½" by fabric width strips.*

4. Cut the remainder of the Jelly Roll strips into (35) 16" E pieces.

Completing the Blocks
1. Trace appliqué shapes given onto the paper side of the fusible web as directed on patterns for number to cut; cut out shapes, leaving a margin around each one. **Note:** *Scraps of the leftover Jelly Rolls strips may be used for appliqué if desired.*

2. Fuse shapes to the wrong side of scraps as directed on patterns; cut out shapes on traced lines. Remove paper backing.

3. Arrange appliqué motifs in numerical order on the A squares referring to the block drawing for positioning of each motif; when satisfied with arrangement, fuse shapes in place.

4. Cut two 10" x 10" squares fabric stabilizer; pin one square to the wrong side of each fused A square.

5. Using thread to match fabrics and a machine buttonhole stitch, stitch around each fused shape. When stitching is complete, remove fabric stabilizer to complete the two Halloween blocks.

Completing the Top

1. Sew a C square to the end of eight B strips; press seams toward C.

2. Sew a B strip to one side of each Halloween block as shown in Figure 1; press seam toward B.

Figure 1

3. Sew a B-C strip to the adjacent side of the blocks as shown in Figure 2; press seams toward B-C strips.

Figure 2

4. Continue sewing in this order until there are eight B strips on each block as shown in Figure 3.

Figure 3

5. Sew a D triangle to each block unit as shown in Figure 4; press seams toward D.

Figure 4

6. Join the two pieced units to complete the pieced top; press seam in one direction.

7. Trim excess strips even with the edge of D on each side using a straightedge as shown in Figure 5.

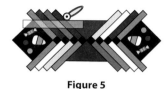

Figure 5

Completing the Back

1. Join five E pieces on the short ends to make an E strip; press seams in one direction. Repeat to make seven E strips.

2. Join the E strips to make a rectangle for backing, offsetting seams from strip to strip as shown in the Placement Diagram.

3. Using the pieced top as a pattern, trim the backing to the same size as the pieced top; repeat with batting.

Completing the Runner

1. Place backing piece right side up on batting; place completed top right sides together with backing; pin edges.

2. Trim backing and batting even with the pieced top.

3. Sew all around, leaving a 4" opening along one side; clip inner corners. Trim batting close to stitching.

4. Turn right side out through opening; press edges flat.

5. Turn opening edges to the inside; hand-stitch opening closed.

6. Quilt as desired by hand or machine to finish. ◈

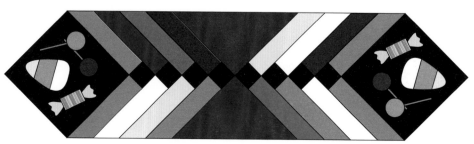

Trick or Treat Runner Front
Placement Diagram 50" x 13½"

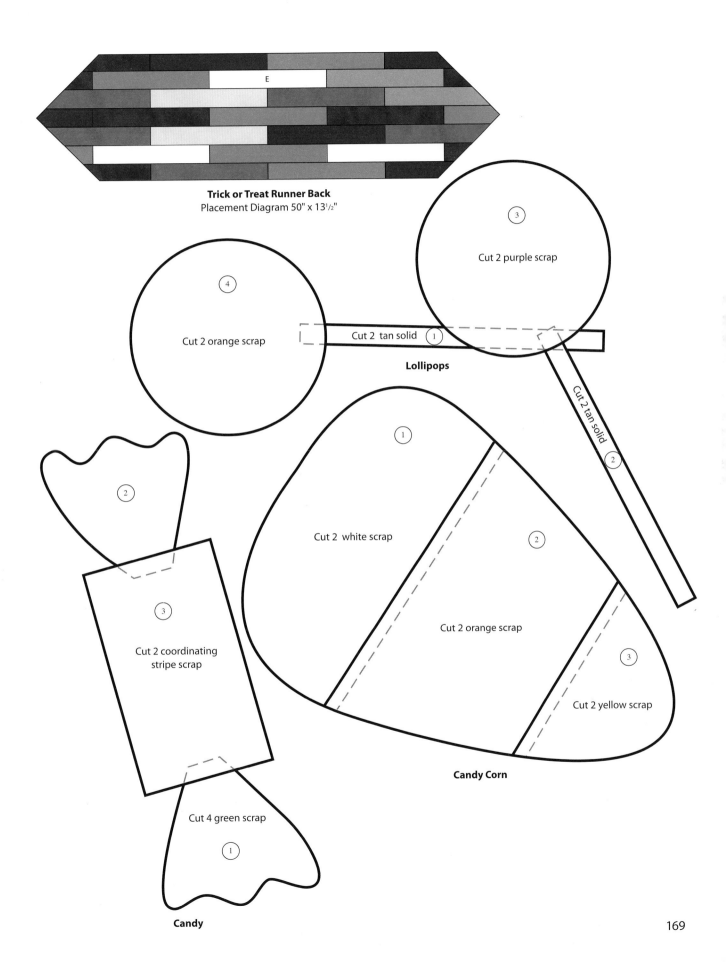

Trick or Treat Runner Back
Placement Diagram 50" x 13½"

E

③ Cut 2 purple scrap

④ Cut 2 orange scrap

Cut 2 tan solid ①

Lollipops

Cut 2 tan solid ②

① Cut 2 white scrap

② Cut 2 orange scrap

③ Cut 2 yellow scrap

② [Candy wrapper left]

③ Cut 2 coordinating stripe scrap

Candy Corn

① Cut 4 green scrap

Candy

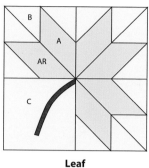

Leaf
8" x 8" Block
Make 5

Blue Sky Autumn

Design by Bea Yurkerwich

Pieced leaf shapes float on a blue background in this pretty autumn runner.

Project Specifications
Skill Level: Beginner
Runner Size: 52" x 20"
Block Size: 8" x 8"
Number of Blocks: 5

Materials
- 5 fat eighths in bright autumn colors for A pieces
- ½ yard blue mottled
- ⅝ yard gold print
- ⅝ yard leaf-print batik
- Batting 58" x 26"
- Backing 58" x 26"
- Neutral-color all-purpose thread
- Quilting thread
- ¾ yard brown ¼"-wide fusible bias tape
- Basic sewing tools and supplies

Cutting
1. Prepare template for A/AR using pattern given; cut as directed.

2. Cut one 4½" by fabric width strip blue mottled; subcut strip into five 4½" C squares.

3. Cut three 2⅞" by fabric width strips blue mottled; subcut strips into (30) 2⅞" squares. Cut each square in half on one diagonal to make 60 B triangles.

4. Cut two 2½" x 40½" D strips gold print.

5. Cut two 2½" x 12½" E strips gold print.

6. Cut four 2¼" by fabric width strips gold print for binding.

7. Cut three 4½" by fabric width strips leaf-print batik. Join strips with right sides together on short ends to make one long strip; press seams open. Subcut strips into two 44½" F strips.

8. Cut one 4½" by fabric width strip leaf-print batik; subcut into two 20½" G strips.

Completing the Leaf Blocks
1. To complete one Leaf block, select same-fabric A and AR pieces. Referring to Figure 1, sew B to one angled end of A; add a second B to complete an A-B unit. Press seams, again referring to Figure 1. Repeat to make three A-B units.

2. Repeat step 1 to complete three AR-B units, again referring to Figure 1.

Make 3   Make 3

B A   AR B

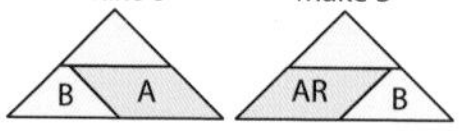

Figure 1

3. Join one each A-B and AR-B units to make a block quarter as shown in Figure 2; press seams to one side. Repeat to make three block quarters.

Figure 2

4. Cut the fusible bias tape into five 4½" lengths; arrange and fuse one length to each C square referring to the block drawing for placement.

5. Join two block quarters to make a row as shown in Figure 3; press seam in opposite direction than the C row.

6. Sew a C square to one block quarter to make a row, again referring to Figure 3; press seam toward C.

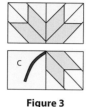

Figure 3

7. Join the rows to complete one Leaf block; press seam in one direction.

8. Repeat steps 1–7 to complete five Leaf blocks (one from each fat eighth).

Completing the Top

1. Arrange and join the Leaf blocks referring to the Placement Diagram for positioning to complete the pieced center; press seams in one direction.

2. Sew D strips to opposite long sides and E strips to short ends of the pieced center; press seams toward D and E strips.

3. Sew F strips to opposite long sides and G strips to short ends of the pieced center to complete the pieced top; press seams toward F and G strips.

Completing the Runner

1. Mark the vein quilting pattern given on each A/AR piece.

2. Sandwich the batting between the completed top and prepared backing; pin or baste layers together to hold.

3. Quilt on vein lines and as desired by hand or machine; remove pins or basting. Trim excess backing and batting even with runner top.

4. Join binding strips on short ends to make one long strip; press seams open. Fold the strip in half along length with wrong sides together; press.

5. Sew binding to runner edges, mitering corners and overlapping ends. Fold binding to the back side and stitch in place to finish. ◈

Vein Quilting Pattern

Tip

Sew a sleeve to the back side of a runner to hang on a narrow, vertical wall space.

~Bea Yurkerwich

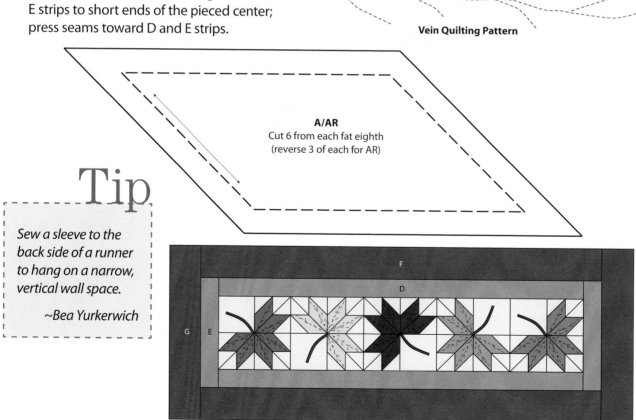

A/AR
Cut 6 from each fat eighth
(reverse 3 of each for AR)

Blue Sky Autumn
Placement Diagram 52" x 20"

Metric Conversion Charts

Metric Conversions

Canada/U.S. Measurement		Multiplied by		Metric Measurement
yards	x	.9144	=	metres (m)
yards	x	91.44	=	centimetres (cm)
inches	x	2.54	=	centimetres (cm)
inches	x	25.40	=	millimetres (mm)
inches	x	.0254	=	metres (m)

Canada/U.S. Measurement		Multiplied by		Metric Measurement
centimetres	x	.3937	=	inches
metres	x	1.0936	=	yards

Standard Equivalents

Canada/U.S. Measurement		Metric Measurement		
⅛ inch	=	3.20 mm	=	0.32 cm
¼ inch	=	6.35 mm	=	0.635 cm
⅜ inch	=	9.50 mm	=	0.95 cm
½ inch	=	12.70 mm	=	1.27 cm
⅝ inch	=	15.90 mm	=	1.59 cm
¾ inch	=	19.10 mm	=	1.91 cm
⅞ inch	=	22.20 mm	=	2.22 cm
1 inches	=	25.40 mm	=	2.54 cm
⅛ yard	=	11.43 cm	=	0.11 m
¼ yard	=	22.86 cm	=	0.23 m
⅜ yard	=	34.29 cm	=	0.34 m
½ yard	=	45.72 cm	=	0.46 m
⅝ yard	=	57.15 cm	=	0.57 m
¾ yard	=	68.58 cm	=	0.69 m
⅞ yard	=	80.00 cm	=	0.80 m
1 yard	=	91.44 cm	=	0.91 m
1⅛ yards	=	102.87 cm	=	1.03 m
1¼ yards	=	114.30 cm	=	1.14 m

Canada/U.S. Measurement		Metric Measurement		
1⅜ yards	=	125.73 cm	=	1.26 m
1½ yards	=	137.16 cm	=	1.37 m
1⅝ yards	=	148.59 cm	=	1.49 m
1¾ yards	=	160.02 cm	=	1.60 m
1⅞ yards	=	171.44 cm	=	1.71 m
2 yards	=	182.88 cm	=	1.83 m
2⅛ yards	=	194.31 cm	=	1.94 m
2¼ yards	=	205.74 cm	=	2.06 m
2⅜ yards	=	217.17 cm	=	2.17 m
2½ yards	=	228.60 cm	=	2.29 m
2⅝ yards	=	240.03 cm	=	2.40 m
2¾ yards	=	251.46 cm	=	2.51 m
2⅞ yards	=	262.88 cm	=	2.63 m
3 yards	=	274.32 cm	=	2.74 m
3⅛ yards	=	285.75 cm	=	2.86 m
3¼ yards	=	297.18 cm	=	2.97 m
3⅜ yards	=	308.61 cm	=	3.09 m
3½ yards	=	320.04 cm	=	3.20 m
3⅝ yards	=	331.47 cm	=	3.31 m
3¾ yards	=	342.90 cm	=	3.43 m
3⅞ yards	=	354.32 cm	=	3.54 m
4 yards	=	365.76 cm	=	3.66 m
4⅛ yards	=	377.19 cm	=	3.77 m
4¼ yards	=	388.62 cm	=	3.89 m
4⅜ yards	=	400.05 cm	=	4.00 m
4½ yards	=	411.48 cm	=	4.11 m
4⅝ yards	=	422.91 cm	=	4.23 m
4¾ yards	=	434.34 cm	=	4.34 m
4⅞ yards	=	445.76 cm	=	4.46 m
5 yards	=	457.20 cm	=	4.57 m

Photo Index

Patchwork Only

Bubblegum & Chocolate Patchwork, 12

Stepping Stones, 15

Blocks 'n' Buttons, 18

Lavender Blossoms, 20

Fussy-Cut Floral Stars, 23

Star Points Runner, 26

Chasing the Bear, 30

Christmas Logs, 34

Add Some Appliqué

Strawberries to Apples, 38

May Flowers, 44

A Garden Square, 47

Green Leaves Runner, 52

Elegant Blue Iris Runner, 55

Roses & Rosebuds Runner, 60

Reindeer in the Pines, 66

Driving Me Crazy Runner & Napkin Ring, 70